Monsignor Klaus Gamber

The Reform of the Roman Liturgy:
Its Problems and Background

Monsignor Klaus Gamber

The Reform of the Roman Liturgy:
Its Problems and Background

**Translated from the Original German
by Klaus D. Grimm**

Roman Catholic Books
Post Office Box 2286, Fort Collins, CO 80522
BooksforCatholics.com

Reprinted by special arrangement with the Estate of Klaus Gamber

ISBN 1-929291-88-4

Table of Contents

Part I:
The Reform of the Roman Liturgy:
Its Problems and Background

Part II:
Facing the Lord:
On the Building of Churches and Facing East In Prayer

Abbreviations

PL: Patrologia Cursus Completus: Series Latina. Ed. J.-P. Migne. Paris 1878-90.
PG: Patrologia Cursus Completus: Series Graeca. Ed. J.-P. Migne. Paris 1857-66.
BKV: Bibliothek der Kirchenväter

Preface to the English Edition

More and more is being said these days about a "reform of the liturgical reform," to use Cardinal Josef Ratzinger's apt expression. Thirty post-conciliar years show us day after day why we need such a reform: emptying of mystery, loss of the sense of the sacred, weakening of doctrinal content, resulting in a liturgy in which, only too often, boredom is surpassed only by mediocrity, not to mention by actual profanations.

It was in order to contribute to the renewal of a holy liturgy, faithful echo of the angelic choirs and of the divine worship which the saints have never ceased to raise up to Heaven for two thousand years, that we have published in French the two studies by the late Msgr. Gamber which are now being presented to the English-speaking public.

The prolific work of this great scholar has remained widely unknown, not to say passed over in silence, even in his native Germany. We ourselves discovered him only after reading the moving panegyrics which eminent people devoted to him after his unexpected death in 1989. We were deeply impressed not only by his comprehensive learning, but above all by the concrete conclusions he drew from it about the post-conciliar so-called liturgical renewal. It has seemed to us a veritable duty to echo, beyond the restricted circle of the "liturgical professionals," the dauntless voice of this "genuine visionary," this "true witness," as his friend, Cardinal Ratzinger, has called him. And we hope that through these publications—in French, and now in English—a frank and constructive debate may begin about the actual value of the principles which inspired the liturgical reform we have lived through and are still experiencing.

Not unexpectedly here in France, the conclusions of our author have been disputed and probably the same thing will happen in the English-speaking countries. But if the opponents stick to the rules of an honest debate, the results can only be beneficial to the liturgical life of the Church. At the time that I write this, the Holy Father has already personally received a copy of each of these two books, and I do not think there is any seminary in France where they have not circulated among the seminarians, stirring great hopes—hopes made more real every day by new events. In this summer of 1993, we need only allude to the priestly orders conferred according to the old rite by two French diocesan bishops: on members of the Fraternity of Saint Peter, by Cardinal Decourtray, Archbishop of Lyons and Primate of the Gauls; on one of our monks and at the seminary of the Institute of Christ the King, by Msgr. Defois, Archbishop of Sens.

And in each case, those ordained are priests who, with the approval of Rome, are going to center their ministry around the celebration of the traditional Roman liturgy. Who would have dreamed this only five years ago? Every year, young priests and religious come to Le Barroux to learn how to celebrate the traditional rite, and discover its splendors, of which we are unworthy depositaries, and of which they feel they have been unjustly deprived.

Should I give a detailed account of these two treatises by Msgr. Gamber? I do not think so: his style is accessible to all, his historical references are precise and his argumentation is rigorous. I would only underline these fundamental ideas:

1. Since the Council, we have witnessed a break in tradition. Instead of a homogeneous and harmonious development of the rites, as was always the case until then, a "manufactured" liturgy has been established.

2. Liturgy is, by its very nature, transcendent. The stability of the rites must reflect the immutable celestial liturgy, and should detach man from a ceaselessly changing universe, in order to associate him with the canticle of the angels: the liturgy ought to be a native land for the faithful.

3. On the issue of the orientation of the altar, which is the topic of the second study, it should be underlined that Klaus Gamber's conclusions agree with those of the greatest liturgists: F. J. Dolger, J. Braun, J. A. Jungmann, Erik Peterson, Cyrille Vogel, Marcel Metzger, Rev. Fr. L. Bouyer, to mention only a few eminent names. Concerning the fashionable altar "facing the people," let us emphasize with Cardinal Ratzinger the serious theological mistake it communicates:

> We risk seeing the assembly turning itself into a closed circle, in the name of community life. Liturgical education will have to work most vigorously against the concept of an autonomous, self-sufficient assembly. The assembly does not converse with itself, but sets out unanimously towards the coming Lord.

As for the oriented (i.e., turned to the East) altar, the Cardinal notes, in his preface for the French edition:

> The importance of this book lies above all in the theological substratum brought to light by this learned research. The orientation of prayer, common to priest and faithful—of which the symbolical form was usually towards the East, i.e., towards the rising sun—was understood as turning our eyes towards the Lord, the true Sun. In the liturgy we find an anticipation of His return; priests and

faithful go to meet Him. This orientation of prayer expresses the theocentric nature of liturgy; it obeys the exhortation: "Let us turn towards the Lord!"

F. Gerard Calvet, O.S.B.
Abbot, Monastery of St. Madeleine
84330 Le Barroux, France

Testimonial by
Monsignor Wilhelm Nyssen

Your life lies hidden with Christ in God. (Col. 3:3)

In 1989, on the evening of the Feast of the Sacred Heart of Jesus, Monsignor Klaus Gamber, Director of the Liturgical Institute in Regensburg, was suddenly and quite unexpectedly called home by God.

Msgr. Gamber's entire life was one of quiet service. It had been completely dedicated to the study of the mystery of liturgy, which he understood as the *constitutivum* of the Church, particularly the modern Church; and he went about his work in a spirit of disciplined self-sacrifice, living modestly, not thinking of or about himself.

How he must have been moved by his growing insight that the only biblical references about the world to come are descriptions of the celebration of a heavenly liturgy, the total consecration of all created beings to the incomprehensible mystery of the Triune God. Thus, all liturgy on earth is but a reflection and an anticipation of the eternal Liturgy, founded on the sacrifice of our salvation by the only begotten Son. Klaus Gamber introduced something new: liturgy as the mystery of adoration, an idea developed from his innermost thoughts and from the knowledge he gleaned from obscure prayers used in the early Church; it was this new way of understanding the Mass that he sought to introduce to the Church of our time.

Through many years of dedicated research, he had gathered an amazing new treasury of prayers from the early Church (East and West), a discovery which he made relevant to our time through his intelligent explanation and interpretation. He had enthusiastically accepted the liturgical renewal brought about by the Second Vatican Council, expecting, as the *Constitution on the Sacred Liturgy* had promised, to be freed from mere ritualism and the confining boundaries of neo-scholasticism. He deplored the (post-conciliar) *Instructions for the Implementation of the Constitution*, because he felt that they had been published with undue haste, that their content was shallow, and that much of it was manifestly incompetent. With great thoroughness and detail, and without wanting to make matters appear better than they really were, he sought to connect the euphoria for change, which could so easily lead to superficiality, with the profound meaning of a real and original source. He did this without compromising with the enthusiasm of the day, remaining faithful to the original form of the Church's liturgy and cult, even though this meant swimming against the tide.

In his career he was both despised and loved: despised by modernists convinced that the life of the Church had only now begun; and loved by those who, with his help, had sought and found deeper meaning and understanding, without, however, believing for a moment that the Church had only started with the Council of Trent. His last book, *Fragen in die Zeit* (*Questions in Time*), in which he critically examines the liturgical issues of our day, is a testament addressed to the entire Church. The bibliography of his works lists 361 entries.

Many unhappy priests, both young and old, and groups of young theologians, who could not reconcile themselves to the official policies and modernist pastoral strategies of their various dioceses, came to visit Msgr. Gamber. They found in him not only a sympathetic listener but a man who would counsel and remotivate them. Large numbers of the faithful besieged him each day at the Liturgical Institute of Regensburg. His incomparable common sense, averse to any form of bigotry, enabled individuals to see themselves in a new light, thus "bringing them to the Lord."

The Holy Father recently expressed a thought in his apostolic letter commemorating the 25th anniversary of the *Constitution on the Sacred Liturgy* that can be applied to Klaus Gamber's life and work: the tree planted when the Church was founded, the tree representing her liturgical life, can only bring forth new leaves if its roots penetrate deeply into the great tradition of the Church. Recently, Cardinal Ratzinger described Klaus Gamber as "the one scholar who, among the army of pseudo-liturgists, truly represents the liturgical thinking of the center of the Church."

He saw his life as a personal sacrifice, quietly entrusted to him. Shortly before his death, a friend asked him how he managed celebrating private Masses, day in and day out, without the reassuring response coming from the faithful. He responded, "Every day I remember and represent the forgotten people." His lonely road of sacrifice has come to a sudden end.

Preface by Bishop Karl Braun
of Eichstätt, Germany

On June 2, 1989, shortly after his 70th birthday, the Lord called His servant, Monsignor Klaus Gamber, into eternity.

For many years, I have followed with great interest the activities of the departed as a publisher and author at the Liturgical Institute in Regensburg.

To the interested reader, Dr. Gamber's publications offer a rewarding insight into the treasure of liturgical history. His great contribution to the study of the liturgy was to bring out the importance of placing it in proper historical perspective. He did this not by merely cataloguing the past so that it may be preserved for future reference by other researchers. Rather, he built up a meaningful relationship between his research findings and the issues facing us today; and by doing this, he stimulated and contributed to the ongoing dialogue among the experts.

Because of his comprehensive and detailed studies of the liturgy, the late Klaus Gamber was able to raise a number of issues about the disturbing changes in our modern liturgy and, relying on his own research, he provided us with a deeper appreciation of the liturgy. He did this with professional competence and spiritual maturity, both firmly founded in his extensive knowledge.

In his critical analysis of the situation we now face, the author was not afraid to take issue with many troubling developments. As was to be expected, however, most of his arguments did not exactly meet with acclaim.

Another characteristic aspect of Gamber's work was his intense interest in the doctrine and liturgy of the Eastern Church. With his writings he awakened a spiritual understanding and appreciation of the Orthodox Churches in many, and brought out the vital link between the Eastern and the Roman Catholic Churches. This is most impressively expressed in his 1988 paper, "Kraft aus dem Ursprung—für den Weg der Kirche in die Zukunft" ("Strength Drawn from the Source: About the Road of the Church into the Future"), a fine example of the results to be expected from the study of liturgical science. In this work, as in many of his other publications, he draws from old, orthodox sources, enhancing our understanding of liturgy in the Western Church, particularly as it relates to the theophanic element (which is designed to make God's glory apparent and perceptible to us).

Klaus Gamber clearly demonstrates the limitations of a liturgy if it is viewed solely as a function. By introducing us to the faith of the Eastern Church, he significantly adds to our understanding and admiration of the full radiance and glory that our own Church should attach to the celebration of Mass.

We are deeply grateful for the multi-faceted and illuminating work that the dear departed has done in theology and in preaching the Good News. I join his friends in hoping that the works he left for us will serve to reinvigorate and strengthen our love of the Church Fathers and of the many different liturgical traditions in the East and West.

Part I

The Reform of the Roman Liturgy:
Its Problems and Background

I

Author's Introduction

It is generally accepted that, in one way or another, a liturgical reform, particularly an enrichment of the Roman rite, had become necessary because, since the Council of Trent, it had become ossified into a form of rubricism. There is also a consensus that the *Constitution on the Sacred Liturgy* of the Second Vatican Council corresponded in many respects to the legitimate pastoral requirements of our time. But no such consensus exists when we look at the reforms that were actually introduced, particularly the new liturgical books composed by a group of experts after the conclusion of the Council.

Some have rejected the new books as artificial constructions reflecting all too clearly the spirit of the new theology and taking insufficient account of tradition. These people maintain that, on the whole, the reform of the liturgy has gone too far. On the other hand there are those who complain that the restrictive framework of rubricist thinking has yet to be breached, and that elements that have not proved their value, or even appear to be questionable, have become permanently embedded in the new liturgical texts.

The ideas we find reflected in the Council's *Constitution* are those of the liturgical movement of the twenties and thirties, particularly those of individuals like Romano Guardini and Pius Parsch—the former an inspired thinker exploring the innermost elements of worship; the latter, an ardent pastor striving to bring the faithful closer to the treasures of the *Missale Romanum* and the Divine Office. Yet, we cannot really say that either of the two was a scholar of liturgical history, and we can say this because neither truly understood the liturgy of the Eastern Church.

Following World War I, when liturgical movements started to blossom, the study of liturgy was still very much in its beginnings. At the universities, professorships in this field were rare. Liturgy was understood primarily as the study of rubrics; and as such, a component part of general pastoral studies. Those few researchers who devoted themselves to the study of liturgical history—the Benedictines G. Morin, C. Mohlberg, and A. Dold, to name but a few—did not, as a rule, hold professorships, and their influence was therefore limited. And at the grassroots level of pastoral care, the results of their research could not have been expected to find much response anyway.

It has only been within the last ten years or so[1] that the study of liturgy has gradually been able to accomplish what it had neglected to do in the past. Today, we conduct systematic research into the origins of liturgical worship, not least because of a growing interest in the rich treasures to be found in the liturgy of the Eastern churches. We also have a better understanding of the importance of Christian archeology and its contributions to the study of liturgical history.

It was at this time of hopeful beginnings that the Council assigned the task of reforming the Mass to liturgical experts. There can be no question that liturgical studies as an aca-

1   c. 1965-1975. —Trans.

demic discipline was still in its early stages of development, and that it was simply overwhelmed by the assignment; and we must also understand that it was in no position to come up with definitive findings in many of its areas of study. In his book, *Missarum Sollemnia*, J. A. Jungmann could only provide a summary of initial, tentative and partial study results; and such insights as there were, were insufficient as a basis for a fundamental change of liturgical norms.

An even greater challenge was presented to the clergy and faithful when the liturgical reforms were actually introduced. Because tradition and local customs had always shaped liturgical worship, there simply had been no time to prepare for this type of change. Participation by the faithful in the formal liturgy had been generally limited: relatively few among them actually followed the Mass in their own missals. Instead, piety among the faithful was expressed in non-liturgical forms of worship, and very popular forms at that. It is in this context that we have to understand and appreciate the person of Pius Parsch and what he did. In his time, he truly opened up new horizons to many people, teaching them to join the priest at the altar in the prayers and the Sacrifice.

Unfortunately, man has a tendency to go from one extreme to the other. If, in the past, the emphasis had been on the clergy performing the ritual of liturgical worship and administering the sacraments, now too much emphasis is being given to the congregation actively participating in the liturgy and doing away with many of the essential elements of liturgical cult and ceremony. Because so many of these elements have been eliminated and are now in a state of common neglect, they are fading away rapidly. Also, we are now experiencing—and this applies especially to worship in larger group settings—a diminishing sense of solemnity. Solemnity is an integral part of the liturgical ceremony. But we are now breathing the thin air of Calvinistic sterility.

In our time it is not uncommon to have a pastor despise the traditional forms of liturgical worship outright, spurning them as outdated. After all, priests seem to say, nobody wants to look as if he missed the boat. And yet, many of the faithful cling to the traditional forms; and the forms themselves live on because of the fundamental piety contained within them. Our zealous reformers fail to recognize the obvious connection between Catholic teaching and piety. For many among the faithful, changes in the traditional liturgy also mean a change of faith itself.

Those in positions of power in the Church hierarchy did not listen to the voices counseling caution, voices which again and again urged that the traditional *Missale Romanum* should not be abolished, and that the new liturgy should be allowed only on a limited basis and only *ad experimentum*. Today, we are witnessing the sad spectacle of so many bishops accepting, without comment, almost any new liturgical experiment, while, when the opportunity arises, severely punishing a priest who, either for practical reasons or as a matter of personal conscience, prefers to offer the traditional Mass.

Nobody objects to the Church leadership adapting liturgical forms to the realities of our time, if this is really necessary. But it has to be done with discretion and great care; and in any case, without a break with Tradition. Even the *Constitution on the Sacred Liturgy* cautions us on this point, when in Article 23 it says, "there must be no innovations unless the good of the Church genuinely and certainly requires them."

With the introduction of the new Mass and liturgical texts, and even more so because of the aforementioned practice of the hierarchy to acquiesce in giving almost complete license for the redesigning of the liturgy, the break with Church tradition is now complete. At the same time, there is no convincing evidence to show that the change in liturgy has brought about substantial improvement in the pastoral care of the faithful. Rather, what we are witnessing today is a large-scale decline in religious life (for a number of reasons). What we can say categorically is that the hopes that had been tied to liturgical reform have not been realized.

II

The Root Causes of the Debacle
of Modern Liturgy

As we have already observed, the liturgical reform welcomed with so much idealism and hope by many priests and lay people alike has turned out to be a liturgical destruction of startling proportions—a debacle worsening with each passing year. Instead of the hoped-for renewal of the Church and of Catholic life, we are now witnessing a dismantling of the traditional values and piety on which our faith rests. Instead of a fruitful renewal of the liturgy, what we see is a destruction of the forms of the Mass which had developed organically during the course of many centuries.

Added to this state of affairs is the shocking assimilation of Protestant ideas brought into the Church under the guise of the misunderstood term *ecumenism* with a resulting growing estrangement from the ancient Churches of the East, that is, a turning away from the common tradition that has been shared by the East and the West up to this point in our history.

Among those who played key roles in bringing about liturgical reform, more and more have come to realize that they are simply unable to control the very spirit they unleashed.

The question we need to ask is: What are the root causes of this liturgical debacle? Any reasonable person understands that these causes cannot be traced to the Second Vatican Council alone. The *Constitution on the Sacred Liturgy* of December 4, 1963 was but an interim step in a process set in motion long ago, and for many different reasons. In the following pages we will endeavor to identify and define these root causes, one by one; but our discussion will necessarily be limited to basic facts.

In contrast to the liturgies of the Eastern Church, which continued their development well into the Middle Ages, but remained fixed thereafter, the Roman liturgy, in its simple, even plain forms, which originated in early Christianity, has remained almost unchanged for centuries. There is no question that the Roman liturgy is the oldest Christian rite. Over time, a number of popes have undertaken revisions. In an early period, Pope Damasus I (366-384) did so; and later, so did Pope St. Gregory the Great (590-604), among others.

In his time, St. Gregory, making use of older liturgical texts, created a new *Sacramentary for the Liturgical Year*.[2] He also regulated the sacred chant used by the Church, an accomplishment that later caused it to be called Gregorian Chant, although the melodies we know under that name today were most likely written a hundred years after his death.[3]

---

2   See Gamber, K., "Wege zum Urgregorianum. Erörterung der Grundfragen und Rekonstruktionsversuch des Sakramentars Gregors d. Gr. vom Jahr 592" ("Approaches to the Original Gregorianum. Discussion of Primary Issues and An Attempt At Reconstructing the *Sacramentarium* of Gregory the Great, in A. D. 592"), *Texte und Arbeiten*, Vol. 46, Beuron, 1956.

The Damasian-Gregorian liturgy remained in use throughout the Roman Catholic Church until the liturgical reform in our time. Thus, it is inaccurate to claim that it was the Missal of Pope St. Pius V that has been discontinued. Unlike the appalling changes we are currently witnessing, the changes made in the Roman Missal over a period of almost 1,400 years did not involve the rite itself. Rather, they were changes concerned only with the addition and enrichment of new feast days, Mass formulas and certain prayers.

Because of political developments in the eighth century, which resulted in a closer liaison between the king of the Franks and the pope, the liturgy of St. Gregory, which had been designed specifically for use in the city of Rome, became the standard of liturgical worship in many other parts of the Western World. The Gallican rite, then in common use, was suppressed. Only in Spain, where the Moors still held power, and in some areas of Northern Italy (Milan and Acqui) and in the Duchy of Benevento, did this autonomous rite continue in use for some time. In fact, the Milanese rite is in use in Milan today.

The adoption by the Franks of the liturgy designed for use in Rome was the source of steadily recurring problems: the "foreign" rite was grafted onto existing local liturgical traditions of many cities and villages.[4] The process was never

3   See Jammers, E., "Gregorianischer Choral und byzantinisches Kaisertum" ("Gregorian Chant and the Byzantine Empire"), *Stimmen der Zeit*, Vol. 167, 1961, pp. 445ff.

4   See Th. Klauser, "Die liturgischen Austauschbeziehungen zwischen der römischen und fränkischen Kirche vom 8. bis zum 11. Jh." ("Interactions between the Liturgies of the Roman and the Franconian Churches from the 8th to the 11th Century"), *Historisches Jahrbuch*, Vol. 53 (1933), pp. 169ff.

entirely successful—and therein lies a great tragedy. It is also one of the root causes of the debacle of today's liturgy.

A second, important root cause is to be found in the alienation between the Roman Church in the West and the Eastern Churches, an alienation that began in the eighth and ninth centuries and led ultimately to the formal break between Rome and Byzantium in 1054. This break, which was not primarily the result of dogmatic differences, was serious in part because it led to the gradual disintegration of a very important element of worship in our Church—that of the early Christian concept of liturgical *cultus*.

According to this concept, the liturgy is primarily a sacred act before God, which means, in the words of St. Gregory (*Dial. IV*, 60), that

> at the hour of Sacrifice, in response to the priest's acclamation, the heavens open up; the choirs of angels are witnessing this Mystery; what is above and what is below unite; heaven and earth are united, matters visible and invisible become united.

The concept of this *cosmic liturgy*, which continues to exist in the Eastern Church, is founded on a precisely ordered, solemn conduct of liturgical worship. The concept ruled out any of the forms of minimalism which, beginning in the Middle Ages, evolved in the West—forms of worship designed to celebrate the holy mysteries only to the degree absolutely necessary for validity. Thus, in the Western Church, the rites were no more than "carried out," rarely "celebrated."

In the Eastern Church, however, the liturgy has always remained a dramatic mystery in which drama and reality were uniquely joined.[5] In this context, we can quote the comment made by Hugo Ball, the German playwright, who is also quite knowledgeable about the Greek Church: "For a

Catholic, there really is no drama. Each morning, Holy Mass is the event that simply occupies him and holds him prisoner."[6]

With the break between the Eastern and Western Churches, this important "drama" component of liturgical worship has been largely lost. In his widely read book, *Vom Geist der Liturgie* (*About the Spirit of Liturgy*), Romano Guardini also drew attention to the concept of liturgy as drama. Today, not much remains of these ideas, certainly not in liturgical worship; the cold breath of realism now pervades our worship.

As the third root cause for the debacle of today's modern liturgy, we must look at the phenomenon of individual piety, which originated in the Gothic period. During that period, the people's active participation in the cult of liturgical worship—when heaven and earth united and divine grace flowed into us—ceased to be the central theme; instead, it was the personal, the individual relationship to God and His grace, developed in private prayer, that predominated.

More and more, the actual performance of the Church's liturgical rites became the responsibility of the clergy. The faithful were present and remained silent observers following the ceremonies while praying and contemplating. Special, non-liturgical "devotional services" were introduced to

5   See J. Tyciak, "Die Liturgie als Quelle östlicher Frömmigkeit" ("Liturgy as a Source of Eastern Piety"), *Ecclesia Orans*, Vol. 20, Freiburg, 1927; see also O. Casel, "Die ostkirchliche Opferfeier als Mysteriengeschehen" ("The Celebration of the Sacrifice in the Eastern Church as the Incident of the Mystery Occurring"), *Der christliche Osten. Geist und Gestalt*, Regensburg, 1939, pp. 59ff.; as well as additional contributions to the subject contained in this book.

6   See E. Hennings-Ball, *Hugo Balls Weg zu Gott* (*Hugo Ball's Way to God*), Munich, 1931, p. 42.

the faithful; they made use of the vernacular, and were meant to reflect *religio moderna*, the new ideal of piety.

The consequence of this development was that the gap between liturgical cult and popular piety grew ever wider. The people were enthralled with all the non-liturgical devotions, which quickly expanded to include many different processions, like the Corpus Christi Day procession, which traces its origin to this time. Also, pilgrimages grew in popularity.

Given this development, nobody should be surprised that what we have here is a clear indication of what one might call a first liturgical movement—occurring during the late Middle Ages! The movement appears to have started at the onset of the Age of Humanism, and presumably was founded on the novel concept of Man's individual nature. The Latin texts of the Mass and Divine Office, and particularly the Church hymns, were now translated with enthusiasm into the vernacular. For example, there is a *Missale vulgare*, a Missal for the lay people, published as early as 1400 in Thuringia, which, in addition to the scriptural readings, includes translated parts of the prayers and responsorial chants of the Roman Missal.[7] Similar books were to follow.[8]

During the same period, we also note a first blossoming of canticles in German. New, popular songs were written in the vernacular; they could be sung during the intervals of the Latin chants of the Mass, or they could follow them. On

---

7   See K. Gamber, "Missale vulgare: Ein deutsches Volksmessbuch aus dem Mittelalter" ("*Missale vulgare*: A German Missal for the Common People from the Middle Ages"), *Musik und Kirche*, Vol. 14, 1942, pp. 121ff.

8   See Th. Bolger, Flurheym, *Deutsches Messbuch von 1529* (German Missal of 1529), Facsimile Edition Maria Laach, 1964.

Christmas Day, for example, it was common to sing, three times, "Praise to you, Jesus Christ...," after the conclusion of the text sequence, *Grates nunc omnes*; or to sing Christmas songs following each verse of the *Gloria*.[9] Also at that time, many church songs for the faithful were written to be sung during pilgrimages and devotional services.

It was Luther who recognized and understood the significance of these liturgical developments; he adopted them and then built on them. Yet, the German canticle was not his invention; nor did he, incidentally, even perceive the need to present the scriptural readings of the Mass to the faithful in their own language.

As positive as these developments may have been at the time, we find in them yet another root cause for the debacle of today's modern liturgy. The popular church song, often of dubious value from a dogmatic and from an artistic point of view, particularly the songs flowing from pietism, tended to submerge the "classical" Latin chants of the Mass more and more, a process which, in the end, caused these chants to be given up almost entirely—a development that we are witnessing today.

The period of a first *liturgical movement* in the late Middle Ages, and of the radical reforms started by Luther and other reformers, was followed by a period of reaction when the Council of Trent established rigorous rules governing liturgical worship; in particular, the rule prohibiting the use of the vernacular.

---

9   See K. Gamber, "Das Erfurter Weihnachtsgloria. Ein Beitrag zur Geschichte des Kirchenliedes in der Liturgie" ("The Christmas Gloria of Erfurt: On the History of Religious Songs in Liturgy"), *Monatsschrift für Gottesdienst und kirchliche Kunst*, Vol. 46, 1941, pp. 70ff.

At that time, the Council Fathers demanded that liturgical books were to be newly published and that their use would be mandatory. This was accomplished by the publication of the *Missale Romanum* of Pope St. Pius V in 1570. A special Church office, the Congregation of the Holy Rites, was established to ensure that the strictly prescribed rubrics were indeed being followed.

The reform introduced by St. Pius V did not create anything new. It was simply a comprehensive review of the Missal, editing out some additions and changes that, over time, had found their way into the text. Even so, older, unique rites, if they dated back at least two hundred years, were left untouched—demonstrating a spirit of amazing tolerance at that time in history.

As necessary as the reform may have been at the time, in a larger sense it also meant that liturgical forms, as they had developed up to that point, had now been made permanent, making further, organic development impossible. Thus, sooner or later, the stage was set for radical change. Before it came to that, however, following the Council of Trent, life in the Church entered a period of invigoration: the Baroque period, the final period in the Western world when Catholicism existed as a unified culture.

It is easy to understand today's level of antipathy against anything associated with ceremonial liturgy, if we see it as a reaction to the liturgy of the Baroque period. Then, the churches were profusely decorated with statues of saints and with ornamentation, and the altars were embellished with superstructures extending straight to the ceiling. Today, in contrast, austerity and realism are held to be the standard for the design of churches and altars; and even to display a cross has now become barely acceptable! If, in times past, Masses were celebrated accompanied by orchestral music, before the Blessed Sacrament exposed to view, in the glow of countless candles and wafting incense, today, following the dictum,

"Get rid of all signs of triumphalism!" the celebrant stands before a bare altar made of stone, which often has an uncanny resemblance to a barrow, saying his prayers and addressing the faithful through a microphone.

Most people in our time simply cannot relate to the liturgical forms of the Baroque. Yet, this circumstance should not prompt us to simply eliminate an essential part of the liturgy: that of worshiping God. To worship—the gathering together for solemn service—is an obligation of man that can never change because man, by his nature, is a social animal; he was created a social being. This is why the solemn liturgical rite before God is not found only in Christianity, but also in the liturgy of the Temple of Jerusalem—a liturgy that continued to be observed by the Apostles (see Acts 2:46). Liturgical worship was a cultural phenomenon in the different civilizations of antiquity, and it existed even in primitive societies.

During the Baroque period, the people, although they were able to partake in the celebration of the Mass in their hearts and minds, could not be active participants in the formal liturgy. Thus, new forms of popular piety emerged, for example, the Forty-Hour Devotion during the Easter Vigil, or the many devotions to Mary. They were deeply rooted in religious practice.[10]

The new forms of piety, together with the formal liturgical worship attracting the faithful with its solemnity and ceremonial splendor, were the pillars on which the Counter Reformation's newly restored Catholicism rested. Yet, we cannot ignore a great shortcoming of Baroque liturgy: the absence of deeper dogmatic meaning, which also affected the

10 See L. A. Veit and L. Lenhart, *Kirche und Volksfrömmigkeit im Zeitalter des Barock* (*The Church and Popular Piety During the Baroque Period*), Freiburg, 1956.

homilies preached in those days. The central mysteries of faith faded into the background, while peripheral truths moved to center stage.[11]

Onto the flowering that life in the Church enjoyed during the Baroque period fell the frost of the eighteenth century and the Age of Enlightenment. People were dissatisfied with traditional liturgical forms because of a commonly held view that they did not adequately address the real problems of the day; there was a prevailing sense of being superior to the Baroque forms of popular piety. A particularly troubling aspect of this first dismantling of the traditional liturgy was that the state had embraced the ideas of the Age of Enlightenment (Josephism), and that many bishops readily joined the club.

In many places, many traditional forms of worship were abolished, at times with the state using brutal force, and going against the will of the people. For example, in the Rhineland, the century-old tradition of the Latin Choral Mass being sung by the people was prohibited, and in its stead, the so-called German High Mass was introduced, often by force.[12] Unfortunately, after that experience, traditional liturgical forms were never brought back.

11 See G. Lohmeier, *Bayrische Barockprediger* (*Bavarian Preachers of the Baroque Period*), Munich, 1961.

12 See W. Bämker, *Das katholische deutsche Kirchenlied* (*The Catholic German Church Hymn*), Vol. III, Freiburg 1891, p. 15: "The following episode illustrates the bitter hatred that erupted among the people as a result of the reforms. In 1787, on the Feast Day of St. John, a great disturbance occurred in the church. The new hymnal was being introduced to replace the Latin choral singing, which heretofore had been the accepted norm. During High Mass, when the school children present were to have responded to the *Gloria in excelsis Deo*, intoned by the celebrant, with a German song, the people started to hiss, and the choir responded with unusual force and vigor, *Et in terra pax hominibus*.... As the disturbance grew in intensity, the Elector dispatched two companies of infantry, the

During the Age of Enlightenment, the purpose of worship was seen primarily as that of instilling moral behavior in the people—which helps to explain why Latin as the language of liturgy was rejected. The State told the Church to function as the extension of its own temporal authority—the ill-starred joining of "Throne and Altar"—by making the people into obedient subjects of the state. That meant that the priest in the pulpit now had to exercise functions that had nothing to do with his office as a priest; for example, he had to explain and admonish people to obey civil laws and police ordinances.

There was no lack of liturgical experimentation then, especially when it came to the administration of the Sacraments.[13] Yet, these reforms did not survive very long. They are, however, disturbingly similar to today's experiments, and they, too, were very much concerned with man and his (social) problems. Thus, Vitus Anton Winter, one of the reformers of the Age of Enlightenment, demanded that all prayers be removed "which place man's hope in God and thus do not sufficiently encourage man's self-reliance." He also declared that, in his view, all prayers making use of oriental-biblical language should be done away with.[14] The newly developed texts were thus imbued with a moralistic tone evident in all writings of that time.

artillery and two squads of Hussars. Thirty ringleaders were sentenced to hard labor; and some among them were never to see their fatherland again."

13 See, *inter alia*, Vitus Anton Winter, *Katholisches Ritual* (*Catholic Ritual*), Frankfurt, 1830.

14 See A. Vierbach, "Die liturgischen Anschauungen des Vitus Anton Winter" ("The Views of Vitus Anton Winter on Liturgy"), *Münchener Studien zur historischen Theologie*, Vol. 9, Munich, 1929, p. 95.

We can conclude with certainty: the preeminent root cause of today's liturgical distress is to be found in the Age of Enlightenment. Many of the ideas of that period did not come to maturity until today, when we are living through a new period of the Enlightenment.

A reaction to the cold reason brought by the Enlightenment was the Restoration period of the nineteenth century with its Neo-Romanticism and its Neo-Gothic art movement. Typically, the Neo-Romantics saw the spiritual ideas of the Middle Ages as the great model to follow and attempted to graft a new cutting from them onto the devastated old tree of liturgy.

At that time, the Benedictine monasteries of Solesmes in France and the priories of the Beuron congregation in Germany came into being. Within their walls, the traditional Latin liturgy and Gregorian chant in its original form were lovingly cultivated; and in these new monastic centers we can also find the beginnings of the liturgical movement of the 1920s. Initially, only small groups of intellectuals and some students were part of this. The Church's Latin remained alive in this movement.[15]

Different from this movement were the efforts of Pius Parsch during the 1930s to create a liturgy for the people. Characteristic of his approach was an over-emphasis on the faithful's active participation in liturgical worship, together with speculation, mostly erroneous, about the form of worship among the early Christians and the design and furnishing of their sanctuary. The beginnings of the vernacular in

---

15 See Fr. Henrich, *Die Bünde katholischer Jugendbewegung. Ihre Bedeutung für die liturgische und eucharistische Erneuerung* (*The Organizations of the Catholic Youth Movement: Their Importance in the Liturgical and Eucharistic Renewal*), Munich, 1968.

the Roman Liturgy can be traced to Pius Parsch, although during the initial stages the vernacular was used only in conjunction with the Latin of the priest-celebrant.

Pius Parsch's ideas about a form of liturgical worship that was pastorally effective, and also more directly involving the people, became part of the *Constitution on the Sacred Liturgy*, together with many of his errors, as, for example, his assertion that the celebration of Mass *versus populum* was historically justified. We will discuss this later in greater detail.

It is no surprise that today's pastors, and among them particularly the young priests who have had no training in the strict norms of liturgy, did not stop with the *Liturgy of the People*, as conceived by Pius Parsch, but developed what in their view were fresh ideas about a *contemporary* form of worship—ideas which often do not conform to traditional Catholic teaching. The Council Fathers, when publishing the *Constitution on the Sacred Liturgy*, simply did not expect to see the avalanche they had started, crushing under it all traditional forms of liturgical worship, even the new liturgy they themselves had created.

Given these developments, the message of the Pastoral Letter of the Austrian Bishops, dated February 8, 1965, sounds rather optimistic:

> It is not going to be easy for many among our priestly brothers, but they will soon be able to see for themselves that nothing has been taken away (through this change), rather, that they have received a new gift. In order to achieve that noble goal, i.e., the spiritual renewal of our parishes, we are sure that all pastors will strive to celebrate the liturgy as beautifully as possible.

The fact that in addition, all forms of extra-liturgical piety and religious tradition have also been abolished, makes it hard to assess the extent of the damage done to the pastoral care of the faithful. We will have to wait and see what the consequences of this wholesale dismantling are going to be in twenty or thirty years, that is, among today's generation, which, unlike the older generation, will no longer be able to live on the memory of what remains as the *quintessence* of our faith. Even the few positive results that have come out of the liturgical reform, which clearly include a greater involvement of the faithful in the liturgy, cannot possibly outweigh the damage that has been done.

III

Ritus Romanus and *Ritus Modernus*: Liturgical Reform Before Paul VI?

In an article entitled, "Four Hundred Years of the Tridentine Mass?", which has appeared in several religious reviews, Professor Rennings tries to present the new Missal, that is to say the *ritus modernus,* as the product of the natural and legitimate development of the liturgy of the West. According to him, there had been no "Mass of St. Pius V" except during a period of 34 years, because from 1604 onwards the popes introduced modifications into the Missal of 1570. It was therefore entirely in accord with the process of development that Paul VI, in his turn, reformed the *Missale Romanum* so that, says Rennings, the faithful "might the better perceive the unimaginable grandeur of the gift which, in the Eucharist, the Savior has bestowed on His Church."

In his article, Rennings has picked on a traditionalist weakness: the expression "Tridentine Mass" or "Mass of St. Pius V." In the strict sense there is no "Tridentine Mass," for, at least at the conclusion of the Council of Trent, there was no creation of a new Mass order; and the "Missal of St. Pius V" is nothing else but the Missal of the Roman Curia, which had seen the light in Rome centuries earlier, and which had been introduced by the Franciscans into many Western countries.[16] The changes made at the time by St. Pius V were so minimal that they can be noticed only by a specialist.

One of Rennings' ruses is to make no clear distinction between the Order of the Mass and the Propers of Masses for different days and different feasts. The popes, until Paul VI, made no change in the Order of the Mass properly so-called, whereas, especially after the Council of Trent, they introduced new Propers for new feasts. That no more suppressed the "Tridentine Mass" than, for example, additions to the civil law would cause it to lapse.

We should therefore speak of the "Roman Rite" in contrast with the "Modern Rite." The Roman Rite, in important parts, goes back at least to the fourth century, more exactly to the time of Pope Damasus (366-384). By the time of Gelasius (492-496) the Canon of the Mass had attained the form it has kept until now, apart from some modifications made under Pope St. Gregory (590-604). Since the fifth century, the only thing on which the popes have unceasingly insisted is that the Roman Canon must be adopted; their argument being that it originated with the Apostle Peter. But concerning the other parts of the Order, and the choice of Propers for Masses, they respected the customs of local churches.

Until St. Gregory the Great, there was no official Missal containing Propers for every feast of the year. The *Liber Sacramentorum* published by Pope St. Gregory at the beginning of his pontificate was intended only for the Roman

16 The Missal was completed by the Franciscans in the 13th Century, and started to be commonly used by the Roman Curia under Pope Clement V, and was therefore known under the title, *Missale secundum consuetudinem Romanae Curiae.*

"Station Churches"; in other words, for the pontifical liturgy. St. Gregory did not intend to impose that Missal on all the West.[17] That it did later become the basis of the curial Missal or of the "Roman Missal" of St. Pius V was due to a series of factors that we cannot address here.

In the Middle Ages nearly every church, or at least every diocese, had its own special Missal unless it had voluntarily adopted the Missal of the Roman Curia. No pope intervened in this matter. The parts which, more than any other, were subject to variation, were those parts of the Order of the Mass said in a low voice by the celebrant (so, the prayers at the foot of the altar, the offertory—also called the Minor Canon—and the prayers before Communion); in other words, the priest's "private prayers." On the other hand, the sung texts were almost everywhere the same within the Latin Church. Only some of the readings and prayers differed from locality to locality.

It was at this stage of development that the defense against Protestantism brought about the Council of Trent. It entrusted the pope with the publication of an amended Missal uniform for all. What exactly did St. Pius V do? As I have already said, he took the Missal already in use in Rome and in many other places and he improved it, especially by reducing the number of feasts of saints. Did he make this Missal obligatory for the whole Church? No, he even respected local traditions only two hundred years old. Such a tradition was sufficient to free a diocese from the obligation of using the "Roman Missal." The fact that, even so, the majority of dioceses very quickly adopted the new Missal is due to other causes. But Rome exercised no pressure—and

17 See Footnote 2, above.

that in an age during which, unlike today, there was no talk either of pluralism or of tolerance.

The first pope to actually alter the traditional Missal was Pius XII when he introduced the new Holy Week liturgy. It would have been possible to move the Holy Saturday Mass to nighttime without modifying the rite. John XXIII was next with his new arrangement of the rubrics. Even then, however, the Order of the Mass remained intact; but the door was now open for a radical rearrangement of the Roman liturgy. We have all lived through it, and we now contemplate at our feet the ruins, not of the Tridentine Mass, but of the ancient Roman Rite which had developed and grown to maturity during that long period. It was not perfect—this may be admitted. But small amendments would have been enough to adapt it to the present day. We will discuss this later in greater detail.

IV

Does the Pope Have the Authority to Change the Rite?

Based on our discussions so far, it is now essential to provide an answer to this question. To do that, we first have to come up with a clear definition of the term *ritus*. *Ritus* can be defined as mandatory forms of the liturgical cult that, in the final analysis, originated with Christ, and then, based on shared traditions, developed independently, and were later officially sanctioned by the Church hierarchy.[18] Based on this definition, we can develop the following premises:

1. If we assume that the liturgical rite evolved on the basis of shared traditions—and nobody who has at least some knowledge of liturgical history will dispute this—then it cannot be developed anew in its entirety.

Even in their early stages of development, the forms of Christian worship were not entirely new. Just as the primitive Church gradually emerged from the Synagogue, so did

---

18 Concerning the official regulation of the liturgical cult, see L. Eisenhofer, *Handbuch der katholischen Liturgik I* (*Handbook of Catholic Liturgy*, Vol. I), Freiburg, 1932, p. 4.

the liturgical forms used by the young communities of Christians emerge from the liturgical rites of the Jews. This observation applies to the celebration of the Eucharist, with its direct relationship to the ritual meals of the Jews, e. g., the Sabbath and Passover Meals, as well as to the older parts of the Divine Office, which are based on the prayer services held in the synagogues.

It was the Christians' belief in the Risen Christ which caused the actual break with the Synagogue. In liturgical matters, however, there were hardly any differences between the Christians and the Jews. Thus, after the feast of Pentecost, newly baptized Christian Jews went to worship at the Temple (see Acts 2:46) just as St. Paul joined four men in completing the vow of the Nazarites and had the prescribed sacrifices offered at the Temple in Jerusalem (see Acts 21:23-26).

Even the one element of Christian belief that represented something unique and new, the remembrance of the Lord in the re-enactment of what had occurred at the Last Supper, was, at least in its early form, organically related to the Jewish rite of the breaking of the bread. And that is so because at the Last Supper, on the night before His Passion, Jesus Himself was observing the Jewish rite.[19]

What has been said about the primitive Church also applies to the early Church. While during the first three to four centuries liturgical texts were not always identical in different localities, the Christian liturgical cult developed quite uniformly everywhere. Real differences only started to sur-

---

19 See K. Gamber, "Sacrificium laudis. Zur Geschichte des frühchristlichen Eucharistiegebets" ("Sacrificium laudis: The Eucharistic Prayer in Early Christian History"), Studia patristica et liturgica, Vol. 5, Regensburg, 1973, pp. 9 ff.

face in the second century when, in many places, including the West (Rome), the feast of Easter was moved in the liturgical calendar, i. e., it was no longer celebrated on the same day as the Passover of the Jews. This change almost resulted in a schism with the Church in Asia Minor. In the end, Pope Anicetus and Bishop Polycarp of Smyrna reached an agreement: since both churches were able to cite existing traditions, each Church was allowed to follow its own local tradition.[20]

2. Since the liturgical rite has developed over time, further development continues to be possible. But such continuing development has to respect the timeless character of all rites; and its development has to be organic in nature.

For example, when under the Emperor Constantine Christianity became the official state religion, the liturgy developed much more extensive and richer forms. Liturgical worship was no longer confined to small house chapels but was now celebrated in splendid basilicas. Liturgical chant flourished. Everywhere the liturgy was celebrated with great ceremony.

These rich forms of liturgical worship led to the development of different rites in the East and in the West. The course of liturgical development usually relied on the faith and spirit of certain outstanding individuals—mostly bishops of renown and influence—and it was their status that, in the end, led to the introduction of new liturgical forms. But as far as we can tell, such developments were always organic in nature, never breaking with tradition, and with no directives emanating from the Church hierarchy. Plenary and local church councils concerned themselves only with eliminating abuses in the actual execution of liturgical rites.

20   See Eusebius, *Historia Ecclesiae*, 5.23.

3. There are different, independent liturgical rites in the universal Church. In the Western Church, in addition to the Roman rite, there are the Gallican rite (now defunct), the Ambrosian rite, and the Mozarabic rite; and in the East, among others, the Byzantine rite, the Armenian rite, the Syriac rite and the Coptic rite.

Every one of these rites has gone through a process of independent growth and developed its very own characteristics. Thus, it is not appropriate to simply exchange or substitute individual liturgical elements between different rites. For example, one may not make use of an *anaphora*[21] of the Eastern Church and incorporate it into the Roman rite, as is being done in the New Order of the Mass; or, for that matter, to do the opposite, i.e., to make the Roman Canon of the Mass part of Eastern liturgies.

The popes have always respected the different liturgical rites of the East and the West, and allowed changes from an Eastern rite to the Roman rite, and vice versa, only in exceptional cases. According to canon law, it was the rite of baptism that decided which liturgical rite applied in a particular case (see C.I.C. Canon 98, 1).[22]

The relevant question: Is the *ritus modernus* a new rite, or does it represent an organic development of the traditional *ritus Romanus*? The answer to this question is to be found in the following point:

4. Every liturgical rite constitutes an organically developed, homogeneous unit.

21 *Anaphora*: name used in the Eastern rites for the Eucharistic Prayer, or Canon. —Trans.

22 The author refers to Canon 98, 1 in the *C.I.C.* of 1917. The appropriate canon listing in the (new) *C.I.C.* of 1983 is Canon 111, 1. —Trans.

To change any of its essential elements is synonymous with the destruction of the rite in its entirety. This is what happened during the Reformation when Martin Luther did away with the canon of the Mass and made the words of consecration and institution part of the distribution of communion. Clearly, this change destroyed the Roman Mass, even though it appeared that traditional liturgical forms continued unchanged—initially even the vestments and choral chant remained. As soon as the traditional liturgical rite had been abandoned, however, the momentum for further liturgical change began to accelerate among Protestant communities.

5. Restoration of early liturgical forms does not necessarily constitute a change in the rite, at least not if this is done on a case-by-case basis, and if it is done within certain constraints.

There was thus no break with the traditional Roman rite when Pope St. Pius X restored the Gregorian chant to its original form, or when he reinstated the *per annum* calendar of Sunday Masses to its original precedence over feasts of (minor) saints on Sundays that were in use at that time. In the same way, when Pope Pius XII brought back the ancient Roman liturgy of the Easter Vigil, that did not constitute a change in the liturgical rite. Even the extensive restructuring of the rubrics under Pope John XXIII was not a fundamental change of the rite. Neither was the *Ordo Missae* of 1965, published immediately after the conclusion of the Second Vatican Council, which remained in effect for only four years after it had been published,[23] or the publication of the *Instruc-*

23 See texts published in *Ephemerides liturgicae*, Vol. 74 (1960), pp. 258ff.; and Vol. 79 (1965), pp. 126ff.

tions on the Proper Implementation of the Constitution on the Sacred Liturgy.

With this background information, we are now ready to deal with the real question: Does the Pope have the authority to change a liturgical rite founded on apostolic tradition and developed over many centuries? We have already discussed and shown that, in the past, the Church hierarchy did not exercise a strong influence on the development of liturgical forms. It simply sanctioned the rite that grew out of local custom, and even the Church practice of officially sanctioning a rite emerged relatively late, only after printed liturgical books became popular. In the West, this practice began after the Council of Trent; and it is defined in Article 22 of the *Constitution on the Sacred Liturgy*. Referring to Canon 1257 of the *Codex Iuris Canonici*, it says, "The supervision of the sacred liturgy depends solely on the authority of the Church, which resides in the Apostolic See and, in accord with the law, with the diocesan bishop (...Therefore, no other person, not even a priest, may add, remove, or change anything in the liturgy on his own authority)."[24]

The Council did not elaborate on what the term "supervision of the sacred liturgy" (*Sacra Liturgiae moderatio*) means. If we consider past practices and customs, however, the term cannot mean the type of sweeping revisions of the Mass ritual and the alteration of liturgical texts that we are now experiencing. Rather, we must understand the real meaning in a larger context: Above all, the Council Fathers were intent on preventing every priest from "devising" the liturgical rite

---

24 The author refers to Canon 1257 in the *C.I.C.* of 1917. The appropriate canon listing in the (new) *C.I.C.* of 1983 is Canon 838. The new canon does not include the text set in parentheses. —Trans.

"on his own authority"—which, of course, is exactly what is happening today.

Nor can the liturgical reformers derive their authority from Article 25 of the Liturgy Constitution, which says, "The liturgical books are to be revised *(recognoscantur)* as soon as possible." As has already been mentioned, the type of revision of the liturgy of the Mass envisioned by the Council was the *Ordo Missae* published in 1965. At the very beginning, the decree points out that the revision *(nova recensio)* of the Order of the Mass is being issued because of the *mutationes* made to the Council's *Instructions on the Proper Implementation of the Constitution on the Sacred Liturgy.*

As recently as May 28, 1969, in an official letter written on behalf of the Pope and addressed to the Abbot of Beuron, who had sent to the Pope a copy of the new (post-Council) edition of the Schott-Missal, then Cardinal Secretary of State Cicognani stated, "The singular characteristic and primary importance of this new edition is that it reflects completely the intent of the Council's *Constitution on the Sacred Liturgy.*"[25] The letter made no mention of the fact that a comprehensive revision of this very Missal was already under way.

Only four years had passed since the publication of the new Missal when Pope Paul VI surprised the Catholic world with a new *Ordo Missae*, dated April 6, 1969. The revision made in 1965 did not touch the traditional liturgical rite. In accordance with the mandate of Article 50 of the *Constitution*

---

25 See A. Schott, *Das Messbuch der heiligen Kirche mit neuen liturgischen Einführungen. In Übereinstimmung mit dem Altarmessbuch neu bearbeitet von den Benediktinern der Erzabtei Beuron (Missal of the Holy Church Containing the New Liturgical Changes. According to the Altar Missal, edited by the Benedictine Monks of the Monastery of Beuron)*, Freiburg-Basel-Wien, 1966, p. III.

on the Sacred Liturgy, it had been primarily concerned with removing some later additions to the Order of the Mass. The publication of the *Ordo Missae* of 1969, however, created a new liturgical rite. In other words, the traditional liturgical rite had not simply been revised as the Council had intended. Rather, it had been completely abolished, and a couple of years later, the traditional liturgical rite was, in fact, forbidden.

All this leads to the question: Does such a radical reform follow the tradition of the Church? Given the evidence we have presented, one cannot invoke the Council's decisions to support such an argument. As we have already shown, the assertion, which continues to be made, that the inclusion of some parts of the traditional Missal into the new one means a continuation of the Roman rite, is unsupportable.

The argument could be made that the pope's authority to introduce a new liturgical rite, that is, to do so without a decision by a council, can be derived from the "full and highest power" (*plena et suprema potestas*) he has in the Church, as cited by the First Vatican Council, i.e., power over matters *quae ad disciplinam et regimen ecclesiae per totum orbem diffusae pertinent* ("that pertain to the discipline and rule of the Church spread out over all the world") (Denzinger, 1831).

However, the term *disciplina* in no way applies to the liturgical rite of the Mass, particularly in light of the fact that the popes have repeatedly observed that the rite is founded on apostolic tradition.[26] For this reason alone, the rite cannot

26 Thus, Pope Innocent I (402-417) supports his demand for a uniform rite in his letter to the Bishop of Gubbio (PL 20:552), a letter that dealt primarily with liturgical issues, by saying, *Quis enim nesciat aut non advertat, id quod a principe apostolorum Petro romanae ecclesiae traditum est, ac nunc usque custoditur ab omnibus debere servari nec superduci aut introduci aliquid quod auctoritatem non habeat, aut aliunde accipere videatur exemplum?* ("Who would not

fall into the category of "discipline and rule of the Church." To this we can add that there is not a single document, including the *Codex Iuris Canonici*, in which there is a specific statement that the pope, in his function as the supreme pastor of the Church, has the authority to abolish the traditional liturgical rite. In fact, nowhere is it mentioned that the pope has the authority to change even a single local liturgical tradition. The fact that there is no mention of such authority strengthens our case considerably.

There are clearly defined limits to the *plena et suprema potestas* (full and highest powers) of the pope. For example, there is no question that, even in matters of dogma, he still has to follow the tradition of the universal Church—that is, as Vincent of Lérins says, what has been believed (*quod semper, quod ubique, quod ab omnibus*). In fact, there are several authors who state quite explicitly that it is clearly outside the pope's scope of authority to abolish the traditional rite.

Thus, the eminent theologian Suarez (who died in 1617), citing even earlier authors such as Cajetan (who died in 1534), took the position that a pope would be schismatic "if he, as is his duty, would not be in full communion with the body of the Church as, for example, if he were to excommunicate the entire Church, or if he were to change all the

know or acknowledge that what has been handed down to the Roman Church by Peter, the Prince of the Apostles, and is kept even now, ought to be preserved by all, and nothing that lacks authority or seems to take its example from another [source] ought to be added or introduced?") And Pope Vigilius (538-555), in a letter to the Metropolitan of Braga, has this to say: *Quapropter et ipsius canonicae precis textum* (that is, the *Canon Missae*) *direximus supradictum, quem Deo propitio ex apostolica traditione suscepimus* ("Wherefore also we have arranged the aforementioned text of the canonical prayer, which, through the kindness of God, we have received from the apostolic Tradition.") (PL 69:18).

liturgical rites of the Church that have been upheld by apostolic tradition."[27]

As we examine the issue of unlimited papal authority and how it relates to the authority to change the established liturgical rite, if the statement made by Suarez still is not entirely convincing, this argument just may be: the already established fact that, until Pope Paul VI, there has not been a single pope who introduced the type of fundamental changes in liturgical forms which we are now witnessing. In fact, we must note that even small changes in the liturgy introduced by a pope have never been readily accepted.

When Pope St. Gregory the Great (who died in 604) decided to follow the Byzantine rite by moving the rite of breaking the bread from the end of the *Canon Missae* to the beginning of the rite of communion, and introduced this minor change only for the City of Rome, this change was sharply criticized. In a letter to the Bishop of Syracuse,[28] the Pope was forced into the position of having to defend it and some other, minor liturgical changes he had also made. In many locations, Gregory's reforms were not fully accepted until the eighth century.

We should point out that St. Gregory never intended the Missal he had edited to be used in other than the papal liturgies celebrated in the Roman station churches, not even

27 See Suarez, *Tract. de Charitate, Disput. No. 12*, p. 1: *Et hoc secundo modo posset Papa esse schismaticus, si nollet tenere cum toto Ecclesiae corpore unionem et coniunctionem quam debet, ut si tenat et totem Ecclesiam excommunicare, aut si vellet omnes Ecclesiasticas caeremonias apostolica traditione firmatas evertere.*

28 See *Ep. IX*, 26 (PL 77:956); G. Gassner, "Vom Selbst-zeugnis Gregors über seine liturgischen Reformen" ("Gregory's Own Views On His Liturgical Reforms"), *Jahrbuch für Liturgie-wissenschaft*, Vol. VI, 1926, pp. 218ff.

in the Roman title (parish) churches (*Liber sacramentorum Romanae ecclesiae*).[29] He held the well known view that *In una fide nil officit sanctae ecclesiae consuetudo diversa*,[30] which translates: "As long as the Church is of one Faith, different ritual customs [*consuetudo*] do not harm her."

The fact that the *Sacramentary* of Gregory later formed the basis for the *Missale Romanum* is due to the gradual introduction of his *Ordo Missae* outside of Rome. People sought to imitate the liturgical rite used in Rome as a way of expressing their veneration of St. Peter, and they did this without the popes after St. Gregory pushing for the universal adoption of his *Sacramentarium*.

For example, St. Boniface, always overly concerned with following the instructions issued by the pope, frequently sought clarifications from Rome, even on insignificant matters. Yet he did not use the Missal of Rome, but the one used in his abbey in northern England. The prayers and prefaces of this Missal were entirely different from those used in Rome. Only the *Canon Missae* was the same. Yet, even his version of that Canon pre-dated St. Gregory.[31]

29 See K. Gamber, "*Missa Romensis*. Beiträge zur frühen römischen Liturgie und zu den Anfängen des *Missale Romanum*" ("*Missa Romensis*: Contributions to the Subjects of Roman Liturgy and the Origins of the *Missale Romanum*"), *Studia patristica et liturgica*, Vol. 3, Regensburg, 1970, p. 116 ff.

30 Gregory, *Regest. Ep. I, 43* (PL 77:497 C); see also *Ep. XI, 64, 3* (PL 77:1187).

31 See K. Gamber, "Das Bonifatius-Sakramentar" ("The *Sacramentarium* of St. Boniface"), *Textus patristici et liturgici*, Vol. 12, Regensburg, 1975, p. 44ff.; see also "Das Regensburger Fragment eines Bonifatius-Sakramentars. Ein neuer Zeuge des vorgregorianischen Messkanons" ("The Regensburg Fragments of a *Sacramentarium* of Boniface: New Evidence about the Pre-Gregorian Canon of the Mass"), *Revue bénéd.*, Vol. 85, 1975, pp. 266ff.

It most certainly is not the function of the Holy See to introduce Church reforms. The first duty of the pope is to act as primary bishop (*episcopus* = supervisor), to watch over the traditions of the Church—her dogmatic, moral and liturgical traditions.

Beginning with the Council of Trent, the supreme authority of the Holy See also extends to the revision of liturgical texts, that is, the review of newly printed editions, and to making such minor changes as introducing the Propers of the Mass for new feast days. That is what Pope St. Pius V did when, following the task assigned to him by the Council of Trent, he reviewed the *Curiae Missale*, which had already been used in Rome and in many parts of the Western Church. In 1570 he published it as the *Missale Romanum*. We can definitely say that the Missal published by this pope was not a "new" Missal.

And we can also say that neither in the Roman Church nor in the Eastern Church has there ever been a patriarch or a bishop who, on his own authority, has undertaken a reform of liturgical rites. That is not to say, however, that over the centuries there has not been an organic development of liturgical forms in the East, as in the West. When, in the seventeenth century, Patriarch Nikon of Moscow changed some insignificant elements of the liturgical rite (concerning the spelling of the name of Jesus, and how many fingers were to be joined together when making the sign of the cross) a schism resulted, and about twelve million "Old Believers" (*Raskolniki*) left the Russian Church.[32]

---

32   See E. Hanisch, *Geschichte Russlands* (*History of Russia*), Vol. I, Freiburg, 1940, pp. 105ff.; see also Joh. Chrysostomus, OSB, "Liturgiereform im alten Russland" ("Liturgical Reform in Old Russia"), *Catholica Unio*, Vol. 2, 1975.

We can conclude by saying that there would be no objection to an organic development of the liturgical rite over time; for example, if, following the decisions of the Second Vatican Council, the Pope had allowed the use of some new forms, *ad libitum* or *ad experimentum*, as long as the rite, *per se*, had not been changed.

Not only is the *Ordo Missae* of 1969 a change of the liturgical rite, but that change also involved a rearrangement of the liturgical year, including changes in the assignment of feast days for the saints. To add or drop one or the other of these feast days, as had been done before, certainly does not constitute a change of the rite, *per se*. But the countless innovations introduced as part of liturgical reform have left hardly any of the traditional liturgical forms intact.

Since there is no document that specifically assigns to the Apostolic See the authority to change, let alone to abolish the traditional liturgical rite; and since, furthermore, it can be shown that not a single predecessor of Pope Paul VI has ever introduced major changes to the Roman liturgy, the assertion that the Holy See has the authority to change the liturgical rite would appear to be debatable, to say the least. At the same time, we can say that there is no question that the Holy See does have the authority to approve and oversee the publication of liturgical books, and more generally, to approve and oversee local liturgical traditions.[33]

---

33 The following point is worth pondering: As already discussed, according to canon law, a person's affiliation with a particular liturgical rite is determined by that person's rite of baptism. Given that the liturgical reforms of Pope Paul VI created a *de facto* new rite, one could assert that those among the faithful who were baptized according to the traditional Roman rite have the right to continue following that rite; just as priests who were ordained according to the traditional *Ordo* have the right to exercise the very rite that they were ordained to celebrate.

V

The Reform of the Ordo Missae:
Could the Council's Decisions Have Been Implemented Without Changing the Rite of the Mass?

Without doubt, Martin Luther was the first person who reformed the liturgy; he did so systematically and for theological reasons. He categorically denied that the Mass was a sacrifice, and in doing so, he also rejected various parts of the Mass, most notably the offertory prayers. He described his ideas and concepts for liturgical reform in his writings, *Formula missae*, published in 1523; and *The German Mass and Order of Worship*, published in 1526.[34]

Luther was astute enough not to make his liturgical changes too apparent at the outset. He understood the importance of traditional forms of worship and how deeply

34 See H. B. Meyer, "Luther und die Messe. Eine liturgiewissenschaftliche Untersuchung über das Verhältnis Luthers zum Messwesen des späten Mittelalters" ("Luther and the Mass: A Scientific Liturgical Analysis of Luther's Relationship to the Nature of the Mass as it Existed in the Late Middle Ages"), *Konfessionskundliche und kontroverstheologische Studien*, Vol. II, Paderborn, 1965.

they were rooted in the customs of the people. His followers were not to notice the differences that existed between the new and the conventional forms of liturgical worship. (Luther himself was actually fond of the traditional rites and chants;[35] he only changed what, in his view, either constituted an abuse or, more importantly, contradicted his own theology.)

For example, when Luther and his followers first discarded the Canon of the Mass, this change was not commonly noticed by the people because, as we know, the priest spoke the Canon in a low voice, as a private prayer. But Luther purposely did not dispense with the elevation of the Host and Chalice, at least not initially, because the people would have noticed that change.[36] Also, in the larger Lutheran churches, Latin continued to be used, as was Gregorian chant.[37] German hymns existed before the Reformation and at times were sung during the liturgy,[38] so they were not a major change.

35 See Th. Schrems, "Die Geschichte des Gregorianischen Gesanges in den protestantischen Gottesdiensten" ("The History of Gregorian Chant in Protestant Liturgical Worship"), *Veröffentlichungen der gregorianischen Akademie zu Freiburg*, Vol. XV, Freiburg, Schweiz, 1930, p. 6.

36 See *Deutsche Messe (The German Mass)*: "Das Aufheben wollen wir nicht abtun, sondern behalten, darum dass es fein mit dem deutschen Sanctus stimmt und bedeutet, dass Christus befohlen hat, seiner zu gedenken" ("We don't want to do away with the elevation, but retain it so that it can go well together with the German *Sanctus* to convey the meaning that Christ has told us to remember Him."), quoted by Schrems, "Die Geschichte des Gregorianischen Gesanges," pp. 4ff.

37 This is described in detail by Schrems, "Die Geschichte des Gregorianischen Gesanges."

38 See C. Blume, *Unsere liturgischen Lieder (Our Liturgical Songs)*, Regensburg, 1932, pp. 9ff.

Much more radical than any liturgical changes introduced by Luther, at least as far as the rite was concerned, was the reorganization of our own liturgy—above all, the fundamental changes that were made in the liturgy of the Mass. It also demonstrated much less understanding for the emotional ties the faithful had to the traditional liturgical rite.

At this point, it is not entirely clear to what extent these changes were, in fact, influenced by dogmatic considerations—as they had been in Luther's case.[39] In one of his research papers, Dr. Georg May, among other things, points to the "deemphasis of the Latrian element,"[40] as well as to the "suppression of Trinitarian liturgical formulas" and the "weakening of the priest's function."[41]

The truly tragic aspect of this development is that many of those involved in designing the new liturgical texts, among them especially bishops and priests who had come out of the Catholic Youth Movement [*Jugendbewegung*],[42]

39   The first dogmatic objections were raised immediately following the publication of the new *Ordo Missae*, in an article titled, "A Short, Critical Analysis of the New *Ordo Missae*," which included an introduction by Cardinals Ottaviani [then Prefect of the Congregation for the Doctrine of the Faith] and Bacci. At that time, a malicious rumor was circulated (see *Petrusblatt* No. 48, 1969) that Cardinal Ottaviani was given this introduction to sign, not knowing what he was signing, because he was blind.

40   *Latria*: the fullness of Divine worship, which may be given to God alone. —Trans.

41   See G. May, "Die alte und die neue Messe. Die Rechtslage hinsichtlich des *Ordo Missae*" ("The Old and the New Mass: The Legal Status of the *Ordo Missae*"), *Una voce-Korrespondenz*, Vol. 5, 1975, pp. 309ff.; Vol. 6, 1976, pp. 1ff., especially, p. 25ff.

42   The German *Jugendbewegung* (Youth Movement) is a phenomenon of the 1920s and 1930s. Individual organizations of this movement included such diverse groups as hiking clubs, folk dancers, the youth hostel association, the Hitler Youth and the Young Pioneers. They all shared, however, a communal-socialist perspective

were acting in good faith, and simply failed to recognize the negative elements that were part of the new liturgy, or they did not recognize them right away. To them, the new liturgy embodied the fulfillment of all their past hopes and aspirations for which they had waited so long.[43]

One thing is certain: the new (liberal) theology was a major force behind the liturgical reforms. (A good example of this is the German hymnal, *Praising God*.)[44] Yet to assert, as is sometimes done, that the *Novus Ordo* Mass is "invalid" would be taking this argument too far. What we can say is that ever since the liturgical reforms were introduced, the number of invalid Masses certainly has increased.

according to which tradition and authority were inherently limiting to the energy and innocence of nature and of youth intent on building a New World Order. Dedication to good, clean living, the wearing of uniforms, proud display of organizational insignia and banners, etc.—all were important characteristics of these organizations. As late as in the mid-Fifties, Catholic youth organizations would, once a month, celebrate a "Youth Mass" during which there would be a solemn procession of young men and women wearing white shirts/blouses and black trousers/skirts, carrying the banners of their respective organizations raised high above their heads in a horizontal fashion, which they then waved and dipped in reverence before the tabernacle. During mass, the banner bearers would be assembled on both sides of the altar, and during the consecration and the elevation of the host and chalice, there would again be a waving and dipping of banners. —Trans.

43 See Henrich, *Die Bünde katholischer Jugendbewegung* (see Footnote 15, above); also see K. Gamber, "Liturgische Irrtümer und Träumereien von der Jugendbewegung bis zur Liturgiereform" ("Liturgical Errors and Musings from the Youth Movement to the Reform of the Liturgy"), *Una voce-Korrespondenz*, Vol. 2, 1972, pp. 249ff.

44 See the report of the discussion between Professor P. Hacker and Auxiliary Bishop Nordhues, *Anzeiger für die katholische Geistlichkeit*, Vol. 85, 1976, pp. 260ff. and pp. 382ff.

Neither the persistent entreaties of distinguished cardinals, nor serious dogmatic points raised about the new liturgy,[45] nor urgent appeals from around the world not to make the new Missal mandatory could stop Pope Paul VI—a clear indication of his own, strong personal endorsement. Even the threat of a new schism—the Lefebvre case—could not move him to have the traditional *ritus Romanus* at least coexist with the new rite—a simple gesture of pluralism and inclusiveness, which, in our day and age, certainly would have been the politic thing to do.

But let us address the main question: was the entire scope of reforms introduced after the Council really necessary? Exactly what did the reforms accomplish for the improvement of the pastoral care of the faithful; and above all, are the reforms really what the Council Fathers intended?

An important concern of the Council was that Christ's faithful, when present at this mystery of faith, should not be there as strangers or silent spectators. Rather, through a good understanding of the rites and prayers they should take part in the sacred action, conscious of what they are doing, with devotion and full collaboration. They should be instructed by God's word, and be nourished at the table of the Lord's Body. They should give thanks to God. Offering the immaculate Victim, not only through the hands of the priest but also together with him, they should learn to offer themselves.[46]

---

45 See Footnote 39, above.

46 See *Constitution on the Sacred Liturgy*, Article 48; also see K. Gamber, "*Actuosa participatio*. Die liturgische Mitfeier der Gläubigen und ihre Probleme" ("*Actuosa participatio*: Liturgical Co-celebration of the Faithful and its Problems"), *Anzeiger für die katholische Geistlichkeit*, Vol. 80, 1976, pp. 238ff.

Since the conclusion of the Council, has our liturgical worship become more attractive to the faithful? Did the new liturgy contribute to strengthening faith and piety among our people? Hardly! Even during the short time that has elapsed since the introduction of the *Novus Ordo* in 1969, our churches have become emptier, the number of our priests and religious continues to decline steadily, and decline at an alarming rate. The reasons for these developments are many and varied, but we must admit that the liturgical reforms failed to arrest the negative trends they were to remedy, and that, more likely than not, they helped make them significantly worse.

We will now show in what way the changes reflected in the *Ordo Missae* of 1969 went far beyond what the Council had intended, and also beyond what modern pastoral care of the faithful required; and we will show that the Council's instructions could have been carried out without substantive changes to the traditional *Ordo* of the Mass.

As already discussed, the *Ordo Missae* of 1965, published shortly after the Council's conclusion, clearly indicates that at least at the outset, a fundamental change of the traditional Mass had neither been contemplated nor intended. In its introduction, it states explicitly that the directions of the Liturgy Commission had been given due consideration and implemented by the new *Ordo* of the Mass.[47] The traditional

47 See the introductory decree of January 27, 1965: *Nuper edita Instructio ad exsequendam Constitutionem de sacra Liturgia plures induxit mutationes, diversi sane momenti, praesertim in Missae celebrationem. Necessarium proinde visum est ut sive Ordo Missae, sive tractatus qui inscribuntur "Ritus in celebratione Missae servandus" et "De defectibus in Missae celebratione occurrentibus," quique in Missali Romano inveniuntur, nova recensione donaretur, quae praelaudatae Instructionis praeceptis respondet.* ("The recently published Instruction for the Implementation of the Constitution on the Sacred

rite had been left intact, with the exception of a few, minor adjustments and edits—for example, by doing away with Psalm 42 as part of the Entrance and Preparatory Prayers and by dropping the Last Gospel.

In saying this, we must add that the cited *Instructio ad exsequendam Constitutionem de s. Liturgia* of September 26, 1964, did make mention of a continuing *librorum liturgicorum instauratio* ("revision of the liturgical books"); see Article 3. Any objective theologian familiar with the way the Roman Church operates would have taken this statement to mean only a limited edit, an enrichment of existing liturgical texts—certainly not yet another revision of the rite of Mass. Otherwise, would the Introductory Decree of the *Ordo Missae* of 1965 have directed that it "is to be published in the new editions of the *Missale Romanum*" (*in novis Missali romani editionibus assumeretur*)?

After all, it wouldn't make sense to order the printing of new missals knowing in advance that they would only be valid and in use for four years!

The only logical conclusion we can draw from this is that the new *Ordo Missae* of 1965 was meant to be published as the new edition of the Missal, as directed in the Introductory Decree (*Instructio*).

Article 50 of the Constitution on the Sacred Liturgy gives the instruction that in the newly edited version of the rite of

Liturgy introduced many changes, of varying importance, of course, especially in the celebration of the Mass. Accordingly, it seemed necessary that either the *Ordo Missae* or the tracts entitled, 'The Rite to Be Kept in the Celebration of the Mass,' and 'Concerning Defects Occurring in the Celebration of the Mass,' and which are found in the *Missale Romanum* should be presented in a new edition, which accords with the directions of the previously commended *Instruction*.") See also the "Commentary" in *Ephemerides liturgicae*, Vol. 79, 1965, pp. 122ff.

Mass, those "parts that with the passage of time came to be duplicated, or were added with little advantage" should be done away with. Unfortunately, this statement is very general and vague. But we can reasonably assume that what the majority of the Council Fathers had in mind were items like the *Confiteor* being recited twice (once during the entrance prayers and again prior to the distribution of Communion to the faithful), some of the priest's private prayers, and the Last Gospel.

The Article's text continues, "Other parts that suffered loss through accidents of history are to be restored to the vigor they had in the days of the holy Fathers, as may seem useful or necessary." What this passage probably referred to is, first of all, the Prayer of the Faithful (General Intercessions) before the Offertory Prayer; secondly, the use of a wider selection of Prefaces. We will discuss this later in more detail. Nobody can object to changes of this kind; they would have served not to destroy but to invigorate the traditional rite, just as in centuries past the liturgy had gone through many organic developments.

We will now examine the different changes in the *Ordo Missae* of 1969, changes introduced only four years after the original revisions of 1965. We will look at these changes as they appeared in the German language version published in 1976.[48]

---

48   While the Latin *Editio typica* of 1970 continues to use the traditional title, *Missale Romanum,* the German language version carries the new title, *Die Feier der heiligen Messe. Messbuch für die Bistümer des deutschen Sprachgebiets. Authentische Ausgabe für den liturgischen Gebrauch (The Celebration of Holy Mass: Missal for the Dioceses in German-speaking Areas: Authentic Edition for Liturgical Use).*

The Introductory Rite at the beginning of Mass marks a sweeping new change. It encompasses a Greeting, or a Greeting of the People, which "may" be expanded to include introductory remarks about the Mass of the Day, and the Penitential Rite or General Confession, followed by the *Kyrie*, the *Gloria* and appropriate texts or songs.

The many "may" instructions provided for in the Introductory Rite, a feature particular to the Missal's German-language edition, literally invite the celebrating priest to come up with his own fanciful ideas of what to do. What twaddle the faithful must listen to in so many of our churches at the beginning of Mass! Incidentally, this phenomenon is now also present in many Protestant churches.

If, in the past, a pastor wanted to introduce the faithful to the Mass to be celebrated—always and still a good thing to do—he could do that before the Mass began. In this way, worship would not be interrupted by what amounts to a second homily. This actual interruption of the liturgy is particularly evident during the Latin High Mass when, after the *Introit* has been sung, what follows is an often lengthy and tedious greeting and any number of introductory remarks, which then lead to the Penitential Rite, or General Confession.

It is certainly important to encourage the faithful to repent their sins more often, which the General Confession is supposed to do, of course. Whether it was a good idea to make it a permanent part of the Mass, and whether the General Confession will over time become nothing but a meaningless formula recited by the faithful, is at least debatable. However, whatever happens, in no way must the Penitential Rite of the new Mass result in the Sacrament of Penance being diminished in its importance as a sacrament.

Liturgical history tells us that until the end of the first century, in the Roman rite, the priest prepared himself for Mass in private, that is, he prayed silently. After entering the church, he would stand at the foot of the steps leading up to the altar, bowing low and remaining in this posture until after the *Gloria Patri* of the *Introit* was sung by the choir. The Entrance and Preparatory Prayers, which developed over time and went through a number of different versions, were not responsorial prayers between the priest and the people. The use of responsorial prayers developed much later, during the dialogue Masses, which first came into use in the 1920s.

The Penitential Rite, or General Confession, on the other hand, was already known during the early Middle Ages when it was called the *confessio publica*. However, at that time, the prayer was not recited at the beginning of the Mass, but after the homily, a practice ended only a few decades ago. The earliest formulas of this prayer known to us date from about A.D. 800.[49] Together with the *Pater noster* and the Baptismal Questions, these prayers are part of the earliest liturgical monuments of the Old High German language.

There is nothing to be said against the Liturgy of the Word, or *Liturgia verbi*,[50] of the new *Ordo* of the Mass. Nor

49 See the *Bairische Beichte* (The Bavarian Confession); see also G. Ehrismann, *Geschichte der deutschen Literatur bis zum Ausgang des Mittelalters* (*History of German Literature until the End of the Middle Ages*), Vol. I, Munich 1918, p. 310 f.; see also H. Eggers, "Die althochdeutschen Beichten" ("Old High German Confessions"), *Beiträge zur Geschichte der deutschen Sprache und Literatur*, Vol. 77, 1955, pp. 89ff.; ibid., Vol. 80, 1959, pp. 372ff.; ibid., Vol. 81, 1960, pp. 78ff.

50 *Liturgia verbi* is the translation of the German expression *Wortgottesdienst* (Liturgy of the Word); see J. A. Jungmann, *Wortgottesdienst*, Regensburg, 1965, p. 7. This expression is not really suitable; a better one would have been *Lehrgottesdienst* (Liturgy of Teaching). In the past, the term *Liturgia catechumenorum* was used. The ancient African liturgical term was *Collecta*; see K. Gamber, "*Collecta*: Eine alte Bezeichnung für den (Wort-)Gottesdienst" ("*Collecta*: An Old Term for Liturgy of the

do we object to the possibility of more than one Scripture reading, e.g., from the Old Testament; and especially not to scriptural readings given in the vernacular, as envisioned in Article 36 of the Constitution on the Sacred Liturgy.

The use of the vernacular for scriptural readings was not unknown in the Roman liturgy. In the ninth century, for example, Cyril and Methodius,[51] missionaries to the Slavs, while working in Moravia, made use of a Slavic translation of Latin Gospel texts. Even in Rome, on some days, the Latin scriptural readings were also read in Greek, for those among the faithful whose language was Greek. This practice continued into the Middle Ages.[52]

However, there is a lot to be said against the new Order of Readings. Following the instructions set out in Article 35 of the *Constitution on the Sacred Liturgy*, it certainly would have been possible to have more than one scriptural reading on Sundays, and a continuing series of readings from scriptural texts during weekdays (*Lectio continua*). This would have truly enriched the old Missal.[53] But why was it necessary to abolish the traditional Order of Readings? We will revisit this issue later.

Word"), *Römische Quartalschrift*, Vol. 62, 1967, pp. 76ff.

51 See K. Gamber, *"Missa Romensis.* Beiträge zur frühen römischen Liturgie und zu den Anfängen des *Missale Romanum"* (*"Missa Romensis*: Commentary on the Early Roman Liturgy and on the Beginnings of the *Missale Romanum"*), *Studia patristica et liturgica*, Vol. 3, Regensburg, 1970, p. 155.

52 Ibid., pp. 199ff.

53 Different medieval Missals show several different readings for Wednesdays and Fridays; see E. Gruber, *"Vergessene Konstanzer Liturgie"* ("The Forgotten Liturgy of Constance"), *Ephemerides liturgicae*, Vol. 70, 1956, pp. 229ff.

The practice of the celebrant being seated on the *sedilia*[54] while the lector reads the Scripture is also an old custom in our Church, which in more recent times has survived as part of the Roman rite in the Pontifical Mass. Again, nothing is to be said against including this practice in the new rite. In the same sense and for the same reason it is appropriate to say the General Intercessions, or Common Prayer, also known as the Prayer of the Faithful, after the homily, at the end of the Liturgy of the Word, as outlined in Article 53 of the *Constitution on the Sacred Liturgy*. This type of prayer at that particular point in the liturgy is common in all rites; and it has been a part of the oldest forms of the Roman liturgy. The single *Oremus* in the traditional Mass, said just before the Offertory, reminds us of this ancient practice.[55]

The Common Prayer has been said from the Middle Ages until our time: the priest in the pulpit would lead the faithful in praying it in the vernacular, together with the *confessio publica*, which we have mentioned already.[56] This practice has, unfortunately, been less than ideal.

Unlike the liturgies of the Eastern Churches and the Gallican and Ambrosian rites, the General Intercessions recited after the Gospel in the new *Ordo* are, regrettably, not laid down in written form.[57] The texts of the Eastern Churches

---

54 The term *sedilia* refers to the seats, usually three in number, for the celebrant, deacon and subdeacon or altar boys. Recently, in many churches, the *sedilia* have been replaced by a chair for the celebrant placed in the center of the sanctuary. —Trans.

55 See K. Gamber, "*Collecta,*" pp. 46ff.

56 See Jungmann, *Missarum Sollemnia*, Vol. 1, p. 602 ff.; see also P. F. Saft, "Das 'Allgemeine Gebet' des heiligen Petrus Canisius im Wandel der Zeiten" ("The 'Common Prayer' of St. Peter Canisius Through the Ages"), *Zeitschrift für Askese und Mystik*, Vol. 13, 1938, pp. 215ff.

and the Gallican and Ambrosian rites could be used as models for the General Intercessions of today. The extemporaneous petitions made in today's liturgy often are the most awkward imaginable, and what is available in published form is of little use.

Saying the Prayer of the Faithful from the *sedilia*, not in front of the altar,[58] is a novelty which stands completely against liturgical tradition. In the past, the celebrant always said even longer prayers, such as the *Orationes Sollemnes* on Good Friday, standing in front of the altar so that he and the faithful faced East.

We will discuss the subject of celebrating the Mass *versus populum* later. At this point we should know that the celebration of the Mass with the priest facing the people was not made mandatory in the new liturgical rite, although the *Institutio generalis Missalis*[59] recommends it.

In the new Missal, the next part of the Mass is entitled the Liturgy of the Eucharist (*Liturgia eucharistica*). Since we are discussing the liturgical rite, we must take note of the fact that the title does not refer to the Mass as a sacrifice, which, of course, it primarily is.

57 The texts of the Occidental rites can be found in K. Gamber, "*Ordo antiquus Gallicanus*," *Textus patristici et liturgici*, Vol. 3, Regensburg, 1965, pp. 30ff., 45ff.

58 See *Ordo XXIX*, p. 33 (in the Andrieu Edition, *Ordo* III, p. 442): ...*et sacerdos veniat ante altare, det orationem: Oremus dilectissimi nobis...* ("...and let the priest go before the altar and give the prayer: Beloved, let us pray for ourselves...")

59 *Altare maius exstruatur a pariete seiunctum, ut facile circumiri et in eo celebratio versus populum peragi possit.* ("The greater altar should be built separted from the wall so that one is able to go around it easily and so that the celebration can be conducted facing the people.") (No. 262) Quoted from *Editio typica*, p. 62.

The first part of the Liturgy of the Eucharist is called the Preparation of the Gifts. While the Latin text of the prayers still uses the term *offerimus* (we offer), the German translation makes use of a lesser expression, "We bring this Bread (or this Chalice) before You."[60]

Nothing is to be said against new offertory prayers, certainly not from the standpoint of liturgical historical development. Except for the prayer *super oblata*, known as the Secret,[61] the Roman rite did not, until the late Middle Ages, have such texts. Texts that came into use later and only gradually were also known as the *canon minor* and did not always use the same words; nor did they always follow the same sequence. The celebrant said them silently. However, we must observe that the recently developed texts are less than satisfactory.

The second part of the new Liturgy of the Eucharist is called the Eucharistic Prayer (*prex eucharistica*). The old Roman title was *prex oblationis* (Offertory Prayer), also known just as the *prex* or *oblatio*. It is in this part of the new Mass where the biggest changes have been made to the traditional rite. Least among these changes is the still ample selection of different Prefaces; after all, the *Sacramentaria* of the early Middle Ages contained a unique Preface for almost every day of the liturgical year; and the Missal of Milan does so to this day.

60 In the American (English) version, the term "offer" is being used: "Through your goodness, we have this bread (this wine) to offer..." —Trans.

61 Secret, or *Oratio secreta*: also known as *Oratio super oblata*, said or sung by the celebrant after the offering of bread and wine, customarily said in silence. —Trans.

However, the three new versions of the Eucharistic Prayer, also known as the three Canons,[62] constitute a complete break with the traditional rite: they have been newly created using Oriental and Gallican texts as models. They are truly alien to the Roman rite, at the very least from a stylistic standpoint. More importantly, theologians have expressed concerns about some of the formulations used in the prayers.[63]

The structure of the Eucharistic Prayer of the Oriental rites, also known as *anaphora* (Offertory Prayer), is different from that of the Canon. In the Roman Canon, the first part, the actual Prayer of Thanksgiving (the Preface) varies, while the prayers leading to the Consecration always follow the same text—thus the name *canonica prex* (permanent prayer), later known as the *Canon Missae*.[64]

In the Eastern Church, it is the *anaphora* that is unchangeable, although there are more than one. For example, the Byzantine rite has two *anaphorae*, that of St. Chrysostom and that of St. Basil. Other Eastern Churches know and use more different versions of the *anaphora*.

Pope Paul VI saw fit to alter the words of Consecration and Institution, unchanged in the Roman liturgy for 1,500 years—a change that was neither intended by the Council nor of any discernible pastoral benefit. Truly problematic, in fact truly scandalous, is the translation of the phrase *pro*

62 Commonly known as Eucharistic Prayers II, III, and IV. —Trans.

63 See "A Short, Critical Analysis of the New *Ordo Missae*," (see footnote 39, above), pp. 17ff. and p. 22.

64 See K. Gamber, "*Missa Romensis*. Beiträge zur frühen römischen Liturgie und zu den Anfängen des *Missale Romanum*" (*Missa Romensis*: Commentary on the Early Roman Liturgy and on the Beginnings of the *Missale Romanum*), pp. 56ff. .

multis as "for all," a translation inspired by modern theological thinking but not to be found in any historical liturgical text.[65]

What is especially noteworthy is the exclusion, without apparent reason, of the words *mysterium fidei* (see 1 Tim. 3:9),[66] words that had been part of the consecration formula since the sixth century. These words have by now acquired a purpose: they take the form of an exclamation by the priest after the transubstantiation. Certainly, an exclamation like *Mysterium fidei!* was not used before in this particular context. The people's response, "...we proclaim your death..." can be found only in some Egyptian *anaphorae*.[67] It is foreign to all other Oriental rites and to all Occidental Eucharistic Prayers; and it really is not stylistically suited to the Roman Canon. Besides, it is an abrupt change from addressing God the Father to addressing God the Son.

The third part of the Liturgy of the Eucharist is called the Communion Rite. It begins with the *Pater noster*, which,

65   In his exegesis of Heb. 9:28, St. John Chrysostom explains quite succinctly: "He was offered but once to bear the sins of many. Why does he [St. Paul] say, 'of many,' and not 'of all'? Because not all had faith. Although He died for all, as far as He is concerned, to save all, His death voiding the downfall of all mankind, yet He did not take away the sins of all, because they themselves did not want Him to do this." Text translated by L. Rudloff, *Das Zeugnis der Väter* (*Testimony of the Fathers*), Regensburg 1937, Vol. 255, p. 180.

66   These words were not yet part of the Irish *Sacramentarium* of the seventh century; see A. Dold, L. Eizenhöfer, "Das Irische Palimpsest-Sakramentar im Clm 14429 der Staatsbibliothek München" ("The Irish Palimpsest *Sacramentarium* contained in Clm 14429 at the Munich Library"), *Texte und Arbeiten*, Volumes Nos. 53/54, Beuron 1964, p. 16.

67   As, for example, in the papyrus of Der Balaisa; see C. H. Roberts, B. Capelle, "An Early *Euchologium*," *Bibliothèque du Muséon*, Vol. 23, Louvain, 1949, p. 28.

following the usual introduction but without the beginning *Oremus*, is no longer recited by the priest, but by the people.

Actually, this practice follows Oriental rites,[68] but its use in the new Order of the Mass is not an adaptation of such rites; rather, it has its roots in the dialogue Masses of the 1920s. Weighing the pros and cons of this particular change may lead to different conclusions: there are reasons speaking for and against it. But it is a major change of the traditional rite, and particularly noticeable when Mass is sung.

The following *Libera nos* prayer was changed as well. The appeal for the intercession of the Mother of God and the Saints has been done away with altogether, and a new ending has been made up.[69] What follows is the people's acclamation of the doxology, "For the Kingdom, the power, and the glory are yours, now and forever." This doxology is used in the Oriental rites, as well, although in an expanded Trinitarian form: it is used by the celebrant to conclude the Lord's Prayer recited by the deacon or sung by the choir. However, since it is recited by the people, and also because of the text used, in the new order of the Mass it is obviously an adaptation of the Protestant example.

---

68 This was also the practice in the Gallican rite; see K. Gamber, *Ordo antiquus Gallicanus 39*. On the other hand, in the ancient African rite, just as in Rome, the *Pater noster* was recited by the priest; see Augustine, *Sermo* 58: 10, 12 (PL 38:399): *In ecclesia enim ad altare dei quotidie dicitur ista dominica oratio et audiunt illam fideles.* ("Every day in the church the Lord's Prayer is said to the altar of God, and the faithful hear it.")

69 "...as we wait in joyful hope for the coming of our Savior, Jesus Christ." Apparently, this formulation is meant to emphasize the eschatological element of the Mass that was part of the traditional liturgical rites. See K. Gamber, *Liturgie übermorgen (The Liturgy for the Day After Tomorrow)*, Freiburg, 1966, pp. 222ff.

Major changes were also made in the Communion Rite and its prayers. We will not take up the issue of receiving Communion in the hand and the problems inherent in this practice since it was not part of the Latin *Ordo Missae* of 1969.

The celebrant's private, preparatory prayer leading up to the kiss (sign) of peace, which became part of the Roman Mass at a relatively late stage (the eleventh century), has been changed in the new rite to a declaration made by the priest or deacon to the faithful. This is then followed by the benediction, *Pax domini*, which, in the traditional rite, came right after the *Libera nos*; and this, in turn, is followed by the (common) sign of peace and the breaking of the Bread (*Fractio panis*), which, in the traditional rite, followed right after the *Libera nos* prayer.

During the breaking of the Bread, the new rite specifies the singing of the Lamb of God (*Agnus Dei*), three times. The new rite simply does not provide enough time to do this, particularly if the "Lamb of God" is sung by a choir in a more extensive arrangement for several voices—because immediately after the breaking of the Bread, there is to be the public invitation to receive Communion. In contrast to traditional practice, this public invitation is now issued before the priest's own Communion. All these changes do not represent a pastoral improvement compared to the traditional rite of the Mass.

The question we must ask at this point is: What exactly was to be gained with all the petty changes? Was it just to realize the pet ideas of some liturgy experts at the expense of a rite founded on a tradition of 1,500 years? Or are these changes to be understood as the deliberate destruction of the traditional order?—because the newly placed "accents" clearly contradict the traditional faith from which the traditional rite has developed. In either case, as we have seen, concerning the pastoral care of the faithful—which, of course, was the

Council's major objective—most of the reforms have proved to be simply unnecessary. For example, to give greater pastoral meaning to the Communion of the faithful, it would have sufficed to allow as a substitute for the Latin invitation (*Ecce, Agnus Dei* and *Domine non sum dignus*), a new formula in the vernacular, on an ad libitum basis. Likewise, there would have been no problem re-introducing the kiss of peace in the traditional rite, as long as this had been done in a form appropriate to the temperament and customs of the various peoples.

The needless destruction of the traditional liturgy also extended to doing away with the *Dominus vobiscum* before the Collect, as well as before the Offertory Prayer and the Prayer after Communion (*Postcommunio*); further, the change from the longer ending of prayers, *Per Dominum nostrum...*, to a short ending, "We ask this in the name of Jesus the Lord"; and finally, changing the place of the *Ite, missa est* from before to after the final Blessing.[70]

In addition to the changes just described, there are the many "may-instructions" [options], especially in the German editions of the new Missal, which have paved the way for the liturgy to be changed at will and quite arbitrarily. For example, instead of reciting the regular Creed, the Apostle's Creed "may" now be substituted; and the rubric following the Creed says that this text "should normally be recited or sung." These options can and have been conveniently interpreted as permission, at least now and then, to use other, "modern" ways of professing the faith—as is being done today by using quotations from Dorothee Sölle.[71]

---

70 It does not really matter—does it?—whether the priest says the Dismissal formula first (which, incidentally, is older than the Blessing), and then gives the Blessing, or the other way around.

Compared to the *Ordo Missae* of 1969 in its *Editio typica*, the Missal's German version deliberately goes beyond the reforms that have been introduced. The German Missal offers every opportunity for the celebrant to essentially "stage" his own Mass. As a result, we now have different forms of the *Ordo Missae* in almost every parish church, including forms that deviate greatly from the standards set out in the official Missal—without the Church hierarchy doing anything about it.

What exactly did the new liturgy do to bring about the "active participation" (*actuosa participatio*) of the faithful that had been intended by the Council? The obvious answer is: Nothing—at least nothing that could not have been achieved without making major changes to the traditional rite. Scriptural readings presented in the vernacular, even the practice of offering more than one reading from Scripture on Sundays; the reading of scriptural texts as serials that continue through the week; bringing back the General Intercessions before the Offertory, along with choral chants; the singing of Church hymns and songs—all these would have been good ways to have the faithful more actively participate in liturgical worship.

But to use the vernacular exclusively in liturgical worship was not a change stipulated in Article 36 of the Liturgy Commission's instructions, to start with; and if we consider the extent of world tourism and of foreign workers living in many different countries, does not insisting on the exclusive

71 See F. Holböck, "Das ewige Priestertum Jesu Christi" ("The Eternal Priesthood of Jesus Christ"), H. Pfeil, *Unwandelbares im Wandel der Zeit* (*The Unchangeable in Changing Times*), Aschaffenburg, 1976, p. 152, where the Sölle text can be found as well.

use of the vernacular in our churches demonstrate a rather provincial attitude? Finally, the relevant document of the Liturgical Commission makes no mention that Latin choral chant should be abolished.

Unfortunately, and in summary, the Council's urging in Article 23 that "there must be no innovations unless the good of the Church genuinely and certainly requires them" has been widely ignored, and the reforms that have been implemented were not confined to what is sensible and necessary. More and more change was demanded; people in the Church wanted to be more open to some very controversial ideas of the New Theology; and finally, the Church was to open up to the modern world.

Although the argument is used over and over again by the people responsible for creating the new Mass, they cannot claim that what they have done is what the Council actually wanted. The instructions given by the Liturgy Commission were general in nature, and they opened up many possible ways for implementing what the Commission had stipulated, but one statement we can make with certainty is that the new *Ordo* of the Mass that has now emerged would not have been endorsed by the majority of the Council Fathers.[72]

72 In spite of the careful advance work that had been done and the skilled manipulation and management of the sessions themselves, the first general assembly of the 1967 Synod of Bishops did not approve with the required two-thirds majority vote the so-called *Missa normativa*, the forerunner of the new *Ordo Missae*. Even so, the development of the new *Ordo Missae* continued anyway. See G. May, "Die alte und die neue Messe" ("The Old and the New Mass"), *Una voce-Korrespondenz*, Vol. 6, 1976, p. 106.

VI

Further Critical Observations Concerning the New Order of the Mass and the New Order of Readings

So many of the liturgical innovations introduced over the past 25 years—beginning with the decree of February 9, 1951 during the pontificate of Pope Pius XII reforming the Easter Week Liturgy; then the "new" Codex of Rubrics of July 25, 1960, long since changed again; then the many small changes made during the following years; and now the "reform" of the *Ordo Missae* of April 6, 1969 have proved utterly useless and indeed detrimental to the spiritual welfare of the Church.

As we know, in its *Constitution on the Sacred Liturgy*, Article 50, the Second Vatican Council ordered a revision of the traditional *Ordo Missae*. It expressed some general ideas without, however, spelling out in detail how they were to be realized; and also, without giving a date on which they were to be completed.

In Article 25, the Council only says that the work should be started as soon as possible (*quam primum*). Yet, not even five years had passed since the Council's conclusion when a new *Ordo Missae* was already completed[73] and placed before Pope Paul VI for his approval. The new *Ordo Missae* was published, after a number of changes had been made, in the same formal and binding way in which, since the Council of Trent, the Congregation of the Holy Rites has always issued minor changes to the official Roman rite.[74]

Since the publication of the new Order of the Mass, opposition in the Church against the new rite has grown. We have already noted that even distinguished cardinals have spoken out against it. In the same context, it is interesting to point out that it is not only conservatives but also progressives who are not at all happy with the new Order of the Mass. The progressives are unhappy because some of their proposed changes did not receive due consideration. For them, all their efforts have turned into a compromise that does not satisfy anybody.

As a consequence, the progressives have simply ignored the new rite, and in spite of all the censures from Rome, will not observe it in the future either. They will continue to experiment, and the liturgical confusion will continue to grow.

Conservatives, on the other hand, do not see any sense in the changes, believing that they are, in effect, destroying the ancient tradition without putting in its place anything really new, let alone anything better. But most of the conservatives,

73 *Missale Romanum ex decreto sacrosancti oecumenici concilii vaticani II instauratum auctoritate Pauli PP. VI promulgatum. Ordo Missae, Editio typica*, Vatican, 1969.

74 See A. Bugnini, *"Documenta Pontifica ad instaurationem liturgicam spectantia (1903-1953)," Bibliotheca "Ephemerides liturgicae," Sectio practica* 6, Roma, 1953.

for better or worse, follow the new rubrics. To them, this is a matter of simply being faithful to their sworn duty.

In fact, it was the large number of conscientious older priests who, in no small way, helped the new Order of the Mass to be adopted so quickly and without much difficulty. This happened because the priests, in comparing themselves with their younger colleagues, did not want to be seen as backward, out of touch with the time. Moreover, the use of the vernacular in the new liturgy fulfilled the aspirations of many pastors who had already introduced this particular aspect of liturgical change in their own churches—except that this type of liturgy necessarily had to operate on two levels simultaneously: the priest at the altar celebrating the Mass in Latin, while another priest or reader led the faithful in prayers from, say, the German Missal and had them sing German hymns. In any case, the clergy were well trained to obey the instructions of the Church hierarchy without question, even if they failed to understand the reason for all the changes. How were they to know the powers and stratagems behind the liturgical reforms!

The Roman Curia's internal power plays were not clear even to those who might be expected to have had some insight into what was going on at the Vatican. Perhaps some of these matters will come to be generally known some time in the future. What we can do, however, is to make use of liturgical research to identify and analyze the sources from which the new Order of the Mass purports to flow. Although the claim is frequently made, these sources are not found in the liturgy of the early Christians, nor do they share a common tradition with the Eastern Church. Their roots are planted firmly in the present.

One analogy that immediately comes to mind is the liturgy used by the German *Altkatholiken* (Old Catholics).[75] There are, for example, the *kleine Bussfeier* (the brief rite of penance) at the beginning of Mass, and the form of the general intercessions; and, of course, the almost exclusive use of the German vernacular.

Another source of the new Order of the Mass, at least as significant as the liturgy of the Mass of the German Old Catholics, is that of the German *Jugendbewegung* and its dialogue Masses. From the dialogue Masses came the practice of publicly reciting what were the priest's private prayers. For example, the introductory rite used to be a dialogue between the celebrant and the *ministri* (the altar boys or Mass servers) at the steps of the altar while the choir sang the *Introitus*. So too were the responses, *Deo gratias* and *Laus tibi, Christe*, to the scriptural readings—in the traditional *Ordo* given only by one of the *ministri*. Further, the *Orate fratres*, which the celebrant addressed to the faithful and to which, in the dialogue Masses, the people responded with the *Suscipiat*, again used to be addressed only to and responded to by the attending *ministri* and could be heard only by them anyway during the choral singing of the Offertory Chant. Last but not least, the solemnly announced *Per ipsum* conclusion of the Canon and of the Communion rite's prayer of peace were traditionally private prayers spoken by the priest in a low voice. Also taken from the dialogue Masses is the practice of having the priest and the faithful recite the *Pater noster* together, a practice quite foreign to the Roman rite and also to all Occidental rites.

Lifted from the Protestant liturgy is the "...for yours is the power..." recited by the people. Most significant, however, is the shifting of emphasis in the new Mass to that of being a

---

75 The German, Austrian and Swiss Old Catholic Churches came into being after the Vatican Council of 1870, refusing to accept the dogma of the Pope's Infallibility and his universal ordinary jurisdiction. All liturgical services are in the vernacular. —Trans.

communal meal (celebration of the Eucharist) in the Protestant sense, the deliberate de-emphasizing of the purpose and function of the Mass as a sacrifice.

The *Institutio generalis Missalis* text deliberately avoids using the word *sacrifice*. It is only mentioned in passing, for example, in Article 2: *sacrificium eucharisticum*. In contrast, the *Constitution on the Sacred Liturgy*, repeatedly and unambiguously, refers to *sacrificium eucharisticum*—so in Article 49 and in Article 55, while more recent references (Article Nos. 282 and 285) use the terms *eucharistica* or *celebratio eucharistica* (Article Nos. 5 and 284) which in German translate precisely into *Eucharistiefeier* (eucharistic feast).

Apparently the designation of the Mass in the first edition of the *Novus Ordo* as "the Lord's Supper or the holy gathering or assembly of the people of God, as they come together, into one [body], with the priest as presider and taking on the persona of Christ, to celebrate the memorial of the Lord,"[76] has its source in the Protestant theology of the *Abendmahl*[77] rite, the commemorative meal. The fact that this particular definition of the Mass appears in a document bearing the signature of Pope Paul VI, and that it became necessary later to correct it,[78] is a painfully obvious indication of how confused things are in our Church today.

---

76 *Cena domenica sive Missa est sacra synaxis seu congregatio populi Dei in unum convenientis sacerdote praeside personamque Christi gerente, ad memoriale Domini celebrandum*, Article 7, *Editio typica*, p. 15

77 *Abendmahl*: literally translated as "Evening Meal," or "Supper"; generally referred to as "The Lord's Supper." —Trans.

78 The revised text is: *In missa seu Cena dominica populus Dei in unum convocatur, sacerdote praeside personamque Christi gerente, ad memoriale Domini seu sacrificium eucharisticum celebrandum* ("In the Mass, or the Supper of the Lord, the people of God are called together into one body, with the priest as presider and taking on the persona of Christ in order to celebrate the Memorial of the

The Reform of the Roman Liturgy

We also need to point out that much that was untested—
for example, the *Ritus initiales*—found its way into the *Novus
Ordo*. This is not the way in which the Roman Curia has done
things in past centuries. Yet this untested material was immediately sealed into place without having passed the test
of time. All this leads to the conclusion that it was the *Novus
Ordo*, and the new *Ordo Missae* in general, that in effect has
forestalled the true and lasting reform of liturgical worship
as envisioned by the Second Vatican Council.

Today's Church has no need for a new Order of the Mass.
What she needs is a flourishing spiritual life. This can overcome the crisis of faith, a crisis that is also a crisis of authority.
At least in part, the responsibility for the crisis of authority
must be squarely placed on Rome.

Life does not exclude order, nor does it exclude authority.
The opposite is true. Life, particularly spiritual life, can only
flourish in an orderly environment. It follows that it can
flourish in a type of order which, at first glance, may appear
to be outmoded—for example, the traditional rite. To make
this rite truly relevant in our time, it probably would not have
been necessary to come up with a new Order of the Mass. We
only have to remember how under the Nazi regime, when
the Church existed in a ghetto state, spiritual and liturgical
life flourished in many, many places. Contrast this with
today. In spite of the new liturgy, the churches grow emptier
and emptier. And still the experiments continue, all in the
hope that the Church will finally "get in touch" with modern
man.

Also, we must not forget this: only a Church strong and
secure in its faith and spiritually fertile will be able to create

Lord, or the Eucharistic Sacrifice"), Article 7, *Missale Romanum,
Editio typica*, Vatican, 1970, p. 29.

something really new and lasting. All else is but an artificial and utopian construct, unconcerned with and uncaring about the true needs of the faithful and their pastoral care; and above all, without any real psychological understanding of the sentiments of the people.

A couple of years ago, several liturgical reformers put together a new Order of Readings for the Mass. Because of their contacts in Rome, they succeeded in having these readings declared mandatory for liturgical use throughout the Church. This product, the work of a small group of reformers, replaced the *Ordo* of the Roman Church with its tradition of more than a thousand years, thus in effect abolishing it.[79]

In principle, the idea that the *Ordo* of the Tridentine *Missale Romanum* could be enriched by adding additional readings is a good one, particularly if we consider that the practice of choosing different texts from Scripture has existed at least since the *Epistolary* of St. Jerome, and even before that.[80] Some of these additional pericopes, for instance those for Wednesdays and Fridays *per annum*, can still be found in printed missals of the pre-Tridentine period, predominantly

79 See E. Ranke, *Das kirchliche Perikopensystem aus den ältesten Urkunden der römischen Liturgie dargelegt und erläutert (The Church's System of Pericopes Taken From the Most Ancient Documents of Roman Liturgy Presented and Explained)*, Berlin, 1847; see also St. Beissel, *Entstehung der Perikopen des römischen Messbuches (The Origins of the Pericopes of the Roman Missal)*, Freiburg, 1907; and K. Gamber, *Codices liturgici latini antiquiores* (CLLA), Second Edition, Freiburg, Switzerland, 1968.

80 See R. Dubois, "Hat die römischen Messe je eine dreigliedrige Lese-Ordnung gekannt?" ("Did the Roman Mass Ever Have an Order of Readings Containing Three Readings?"), *Heiliger Dienst*, Vol. 18, 1964, pp. 129ff.

in German-speaking areas and also in the Patriarchy of Aquileia.[81]

As far as the traditional Roman rite is concerned, there would have been nothing wrong with introducing specific additional texts for the week's feast days, and adding reading cycles on Sundays. Finally, we can observe that the Order of Readings for Sundays was established relatively late in liturgical history, as documented by the *Würzburger Epistelliste* (*Epistolary of Würzburg*) of c. 700.[82]

Aside from the fact that the new Order of Readings has completely replaced the old one, abruptly breaking with ancient tradition, many liturgical experts have criticized the selection of the new texts as showing a marked preference for their exegetic character and not giving due consideration to existing liturgical rules and customs, which always governed the way in which the Church selected passages from Scripture. Stonner goes even so far as to suggest that in some instances, "scriptural texts used in the liturgy have gone through a process of rewriting."[83] Moreover, it has always been important to choose carefully the words used at the beginning and end of a particular text selected for the reading, since these words tend to carry a special meaning. For example, quite unworkable (and ridiculous) is the ending

81 The Order of the Missal of Constance of the year 1504 had been edited in this way; see E. Gruber, "Vergessene Konstanzer Liturgie?" ("The Liturgy of Constance—Now Forgotten?"), *Ephemerides liturgicae*, Vol. 70, 1956, pp. 229ff.

82 See *CLLA*, No. 1001, Footnote 67, above. See also G. Kunze, "Das Rätsel der Würzburger Epistelliste" ("The Mystery of the Würzburger Epistelliste"), *Colligere Fragmenta* in *Texte und Arbeiten*, Second Addendum, Beuron, 1952, pp. 191ff.

83 A. Stonner, *Bibellesung mit der katholischen Jugend (Bible Readings with Catholic Youth)*, Paderborn, 1935, p. 188.

currently in use as part of the scriptural readings for the First Sunday in Lent (Reading Cycle for Year A): "Then the eyes of both of them were opened and they knew that they were naked," to which the faithful are expected to respond, "Thanks be to God!" The selection of texts from the Gospel used for the readings used to derive from the premise that there should be a meaningful relationship between these texts and the particular mystery being celebrated in the Mass—a premise frequently cited in Parsch's book, *Jahr des Heils* (*The Year of Salvation*). In the Introduction, Parsch says:

> In the Gospel, Christ appears and speaks to us. We must understand the Gospel not so much as a Lesson being taught, but as the Epiphany [appearance] of Christ. At the same time and in most instances, the Gospel introduces the central part of the drama of mystery.[84]

In contrast, the new Order of Readings, following the concepts on which Protestant worship is based, is designed primarily to serve the purpose of teaching the faithful and to provide for their *edification*. It is obvious that exegetes, not liturgists, developed the new Order of Readings. What the exegetes apparently failed to consider is that most among the faithful simply do not have the necessary background and knowledge to understand, let alone appreciate, certain passages from Scripture; that they know little about salvation history prior to Christ; and that, therefore, there is little in the Pentateuch or in the Books of Kings that would have any real meaning to them. As a consequence, readings from the Old Testament selected in the new Order of Readings for week-

---

84 Pius Parsch, *Jahr des Heils* (*The Year of Salvation*), Tenth Edition, Klosterneuburg, 1932, p. 16.

day use usually go beyond the comprehension of the faith-ful,[85] and are therefore simply omitted altogether.

Those involved in liturgical research know—or at least they should know—of the many Orders of Readings used now and in the past by the Eastern and the Western churches. They should also know what rules applied in selecting passages from Scripture to be used in the liturgy. It is surprising, indeed, that so little effort was made to refer to and make use of these older versions of the Orders of Readings, which in part go back to the fourth and fifth centuries. What a wealth of inspiration could have been found in them! But then, it is only too clear that Church tradition was deliberately rejected.

The oldest part of the *Great Lectionary of the Church of Jerusalem* goes back to the fifth century, passed down to us through the later Georgian manuscripts.[86] A Coptic *Evangelistarium*[87] also appears to be of ancient origin. So do a number of old lectionaries from Egypt still waiting to be studied.[88] A.

85 See Th. Kurrus, "Kritisches zum neuen Schriftlesungsplan" ("Critical Remarks about the New Order of Readings"), *Anzeiger für die katholische Geistlichkeit*, Vol. 81, 1972, pp. 81ff.

86 See the Latin translation by M. Tarschnischvili in "Le Grand Lectionaire de l'église de Jérusalem, Ve-VIIIe siècle" ("The Great Lectionary of the Church of Jerusalem, 5th to 8th Centuries"), *Corpus scriptorum christianorum orientalium*, Vols. 189 and 205, Louvain, 1959/60.

87 Published by J. Drescher, "A Coptic Lectionary Fragment," *Annales du Services des Antiquités de l'Egypte*, Vol. 51, pp. 247ff.; see also K. Gamber, "Eine alte Evangelienliste aus Ägypten" ("An Ancient Evangelistarium from Egypt"), *Heiliger Dienst*, Vol. 29, 1975, pp. 124ff.

88 See K. Gamber, "Fragmente eines griechischen Perikopenbuches des 5. Jh. aus Ägypten" ("Fragments of a Greek Book of Pericopes of the Fifth Century from Egypt"), *Oriens Christianus*, Vol. 44, 1960, pp. 75ff.

Baumstark has been involved in research on the most ancient Syriac Orders of Readings.[89]

From Occidental sources we can cite, among others, the *Evangelistarium of Aquileia;*[90] also, the old *Campanian Order of Readings,* as it has been passed down to us in the famous *Code Fuldensis* (Epistolary); and a number of Anglo-Saxon Evangelaries.[91] To complete the list of only the most ancient documents, we must add an Epistolary that in its original form goes back to the time of St. Peter Chrysologus, who died in 450.[92] Somewhat more recent are the surviving lectionaries of the Church's old rite of Milan, the old Gallican rite and the old Spanish rite.[93]

For the Roman Church, there is an Epistolary known as the *Liber comitis.* It was probably arranged by St. Jerome, who died in 419 or 420. This book was first cited in documents in 471 and has been passed down to us in the already cited

89 See A. Baumstark, "Nichtevangelische syrische Perikopenordnung des ersten Jahrtausends" ("The Non-Gospel Syriac Order of Pericopes of the First Millennium"), *Liturgiegeschichtliche Forschungen,* Vol. 3, Münster, 1921.

90 See K. Gamber, "Die älteste abendländische Evangelien-Perikopenliste" ("The Most Ancient Occidental Evangelistarium"), *Münchener Theol. Zeitschrift,* Vol. 13, 1962, pp. 181-201; see also *CLLA,* No. 245. About an early Bavarian Epistolary, see K. Gamber, "Reste einer gallikanischen Epistelliste" ("Fragments of a Gallican Epistolary"), *Rev. bénéd.,* Vol. 88, 1978, pp. 111ff.

91 See K. Gamber, "Die kampanische Lektionsordnung" ("The Order of Readings of Campano"), *Sacris erudiri,* Vol. 13, 1962, pp. 326ff.; see also *CLLA,* No. 401 and 405/406.

92 See K. Gamber, "Eine altravenatische Epistelliste" ("An Ancient Epistolary from Ravenna"), *Liturgisches Jahrbuch,* Vol. 8, 1958, pp. 73ff.; see also *CLLA,* No. 242 and compare with No. 240.

93 See G. Kunze, *Die gottesdienstliche Schriftlesung, Teil I (The Order of Readings for the Mass, Part I),* Göttingen, 1947, pp. 25ff.

Würzburger Epistelliste (*Epistolary of Würzburg*) of c. 700.[94] It forms the foundation for the pericopes of the *Missale Romanum* that are not taken from the Gospels, together with the ancient *Roman Evangelistarium* (*Capitulare Evangeliorum*)[95] which, however, was more extensively developed than the Order of Readings appearing in the later Missal.[96]

As did the other liturgical reforms introduced in the aftermath of the Second Vatican Council, the development of a new Order of Readings represented a break with ancient Church tradition, a tradition that, at least in part, goes back 1,500 years. Yet the new Order of Readings was unable to come up with something better to take the place of the traditional *Ordo*. In retrospect, it would probably have been wiser—not least from a pastoral perspective—to retain the traditional *Ordo* of the *Missale Romanum* while, as an element of the reform, offering additional texts *ad libitum* from which to choose.

This would have been a true reform indeed; that is, a return to the original, ancient form of liturgy. It would not

94 See K. Gamber, "Sakramentarstudien" ("Studies of *Sacra-mentaria*"), *Studia patristica et liturgica*, Vol. 7, Regensburg, 1978, pp. 19ff.

95 See Th. Klauser, "Das römische *Capitulare Evangeliorum*. Texte und Untersuchungen zu seiner ältesten Geschichte" ("The Roman *Capitulare Evangeliorum*: Texts and Investigations of its Most Ancient History"), *Liturgiegeschichtliche Quellen und Forschungen*, Vol. 28, Münster, 1935.

96 Referring to the *Capitulare Evangeliorum*, there are several different Evangeliaries which, although they do not contain the same selection of texts as the *Capitulare Evangeliorum*, do show the complete text of their pericopes. Among them, one of the most ancient is the Evangelary of Müstair. See also K. Gamber, S. Rehle, "Das Evangelistar von Müstair" ("The *Evangelistarium* of Müstair"), *Zeitschrift für schweizerische Kirchengeschichte*, Vol. 67, 1973, pp. 258ff.

have destroyed something old and precious that had passed the test of time. As it is, the traditions of the Western and the Eastern churches have been abandoned to follow the dangerous road of experimentation, without giving us the option to return to the traditional way, and to do so easily and expeditiously.

Considering all this, it should come as no surprise when "progressive" pastors carry "liturgical renewal" yet a step further, substituting for the texts taken from Scripture passages from the writings of Karl Marx and Mao Tse-Tung; or even, if it is "relevant," to read something from a newspaper. It is quite easy to destroy an old order, but to create a new one is something else again.

VII

Celebrating the Mass *Versus Populum*: Liturgical and Sociological Aspects

In his *Guidelines for the Design of the House of God According to the Spirit of Roman Liturgy* (1949), T. Klauser writes:

> There are some indications that in the church of the future, the celebrant priest will again be standing behind the altar, facing the people, as this is still done today in the ancient Roman basilicas; it appears that this approach is necessary because of the commonly felt desire to give a clearer expression to the concept of a eucharistic assembly around the table.

What Klauser then thought desirable has become the accepted standard. Indeed, in accepting it, it is commonly believed that a tradition of the early Christians has been restored. In response, we can say and convincingly demonstrate that neither in the Eastern nor the Western Church was there ever a celebration *versus populum*—rather, there was only the practice of turning towards the East while praying.[97]

Martin Luther was the first person to demand that the priest at the altar face the people.[98] As far as we know, Luther himself never followed his own demand, and in the different Protestant churches, it was met only by individual pastors, especially in the Protestant Reformed Churches.[99] Celebrating the Mass *versus populum*, now almost universally prac-

97 See the detailed study by K. Gamber, *"Conversi ad Dominum.* Die Hinwendung von Priester und Volk nach Osten bei der Messfeier im 4. und 5. Jahrhundert" (*"Conversi Ad Dominum*: The Turning Towards the East by the Priest and Faithful During the Celebration of the Mass During the 4th and 5th Centuries"), *Römische Quartalschrift*, Vol. 67, 1972, pp. 49ff.; also "Liturgie und Kirchenbau" ("Liturgy and the Building of Churches"), *Studia patristica et liturgica*, Vol. 6, Regensburg, 1976, pp. 7ff.

98 In his little book, *Deutsche Messe und Ordnung des Gottesdienstes* (*The German Mass and Order of Worship*), published in 1526, he writes at the beginning of the chapter entitled, "Des Sonntags für die Laien": "Da lassen wir die Messgewänder, Altar, Lichter noch bleiben, bis sie alle werden oder uns gefällt zu ändern. Wer aber hier anders verfahren will, lassen wir geschehen. Aber in der rechten Messe unter eitel Christen müsste der Altar nicht so bleiben und der Priester sich immer zum Volk kehren, wie ohne Zweifel Christus beim Abendmahl getan hat. Nun, das erharre seiner Zeit." ("Let all the vestments, the altar, the candles be, until they get used up, or we decide to change them. And if somebody wants to do things differently, let him do it. But for the real Mass among true Christians, the altar should not remain in its current form and the priest should always face the people—as we can assume without question Christ did during the Last Supper. Well, all this will come to pass in time."); see also K. Gamber, "Die Zelebration *versus populum* eine Erfindung und Forderung Martin Luthers" ("The Celebration *versus populum*: An Invention and Demand Made by Martin Luther"), *Anzeiger für die katholische Geistlichkeit*, Vol. 79, 1970, pp. 355ff.; republished in K. Gamber, *Ritus modernus. Gesammelte Aufsätze zur Litugiereform* (*Ritus Modernus: Collected Essays on Liturgical Reform*), Regensburg, 1972, pp. 21-29.

99 See Fr. Schulz, "Das Mahl der Brüder" ("The Meal of the Brothers"), *Jahrbuch für Liturgik und Hymnologie*, Vol. 15, 1970, p. 34, Footnote 8: "So liess seinerzeit Martin Bucer in Strassburg Abendmahlstische aufstellen, 'dass der diener das angesicht gegen das Volck wendet.'" ("Thus, at that time, Martin Bucer had tables for the Lord's Supper set up in such a way 'that the minister faced the people.'")

ticed in Roman Catholic churches, is a very recent development, while the Eastern Churches and also many Protestant
Churches continue the old tradition.

In the Eastern Church, the celebration *versus populum* has
never been practiced; in fact, there is not even a term to
describe it. The deepest reverence is shown to the altar's front
side: only the priest, and next to him, the deacon, is allowed
to stand there. In the sanctuary, behind the iconostasis, it is
only the celebrant who can pass in front of the altar. Also, we
should note that during a concelebration, which, as we know,
has a long tradition in the Eastern Church, the main celebrant
stands, as always, with his back to the people, while the
co-celebrating priests position themselves to his left and
right. In no case, however, do they stand at the altar's back
side, that is, its East side.

The practice of celebrating Mass facing the people came
to us as part of the *Jugendbewegung*, during the 1920s, when
it was popular to celebrate the Eucharist in small groups. The
liturgical movement, with Pius Parsch leading the charge,
also promoted this practice. Because people saw that in some
ancient Roman basilicas the altar was also facing *versus populum* they believed that their current practice was, in fact, the
revival of an early Christian tradition. It seems that what
these people overlooked was that, unlike other churches,[100]
in these basilicas it was not the apse that was facing East, but
the entrance door.

100 There are few churches outside Rome that have their entrance on
the East side. Best known among them is the basilica in Tyre that
has been described by Eusebius. As was this basilica, all others
designed in the same way were built by Emperor Constantine, or
by his mother, St. Helena. See G. Kunze, *Lehre, Gottesdienst,
Kirchenbau in ihren gegenseitigen Beziehungen (Teaching, Worship, the
Building of Churches and How They are Mutually Dependant and
Related)*, Vol. I, Göttingen, 1949, pp. 51ff., especially p. 53.

What in the early Church and during the Middle Ages determined the position of the altar was that it faced East. To quote St. Augustine: "When we rise to pray, we turn East, where heaven begins. And we do this not because God is there, as if He had moved away from the other directions on earth..., but rather to help us remember to turn our mind towards a higher order, that is, to God."[101] This quotation shows that the Christians of those early days, after listening to the homily, would rise for the prayer which followed, and turn towards the East. St. Augustine always refers to this turning to the East in prayer at the end of his homilies, using a set formula, *Conversi ad Dominum* ("turn to face the Lord").[102]

In his pioneering book, *Sol salutis*, Dölger advances the argument that the people's response, *habemus ad Dominum*, following the priest's call of *Sursum corda*, also indicates that the faithful have turned towards the East, by pointing to the fact that in some oriental liturgies, the deacon specifically calls out for this to happen.[103] This applies to the Coptic Basilius liturgy, which, at the beginning of its *anaphora*, says, "Come close, you men, stand in reverence and look towards the East!"; or the Egyptian Marcus liturgy, which contains a similar call, "Look towards the East!" which is part of the

---

101 Augustine, *De sermone domini in monte* II.18, PL 34:1277.

102 See "*Sol salutis*. Gebet und Gesang im christlichen Altertum mit besonderer Rücksicht auf die Ostung in Gebet und Liturgie" ("Sol salutis: Prayer and Hymns in Christian Antiquity with Special Emphasis on Facing East in Prayer and Liturgy"), *Liturgiegeschichtliche Quellen und Forschungen*, Vols. 4/5, First Edition, Münster, 1920, Second Edition, 1925, pp. 254ff. We are quoting from the First Edition which is more widely available.

103 See J. Dölger, *Sol salutis*, pp. 251, 256.

Eucharistic prayer recited prior to the part leading up to the *Sanctus*.

Also, in the short description of the liturgy contained in the second book of the *Apostolic Constitution* issued at the end of the fourth century, we find the practice of rising for prayer and facing East.[104] The eighth book quotes the actual call by the deacon, "Stand upright, towards the Lord!"[105] This would indicate that in the early Church, the turning towards the Lord and the turning towards the East were one and the same.[106]

Dölger has shown that the custom of praying in the direction of sunrise is an ancient one, practiced by Jews and pagans alike. The custom was adopted early on by the Christians. For example, to face East in prayer was a common practice for Tertullian, as early as 197. In his *Apologeticum* (c. 16) he speaks about the Christians "praying in the direction of the rising sun."[107]

The sun served as a symbol for the Lord having ascended to heaven and of His return from there. In order that the rays of the rising sun would stream into the inside of the church during Mass, the church entrance was placed at the Eastern side of the building, which meant that the doors had to

104 *Const. Apost.* II, 57, 14; in the Funk edition, p. 165; see also J. Dölger, *Sol salutis*, pp. 127ff.

105 *Const. Apost.* VIII, 12, 2; in the Funk edition, p. 494.

106 See J. Dölger, *Sol salutis*, pp. 250ff.; see also E. Peterson, *Frühkirche, Judentum und Gnosis (The Early Church, Judaism and Gnosis)*, Rome, 1959, pp. 15ff. ("The Cross and the Prayer Facing East. Attention is drawn to the fact that a cross affixed to the East wall indicated the direction of prayer. Such a cross was found on the wall of a room in a house in Herculaneum."), Munich, 1951, Illustration 29, following p. 96.

107 See J. Dölger, *Sol salutis*, p. 103.

remain open and the direction of prayer was necessarily towards the doors; this was done in Rome during the fourth and fifth centuries; at times, this practice was observed outside of Rome, as well.[108]

As we have already observed, in this type of setting, the liturgy was celebrated from behind the altar in order to face East when offering the Sacrifice. But this did not represent, as might be implied, a celebration *versus populum*, since the faithful were facing East in prayer as well. Thus, even in the basilicas just described, the celebration of the Eucharist did not entail the priest and the faithful facing one another. During Mass, the faithful, men separated from women, were assembled in the two side naves, with curtains normally hanging between the columns.[109]

The center nave was used for the solemn entrance procession of the celebrant and his assistants to the altar, and the choir was situated there as well. Even if we take the hypothetical case that the early Christians in the old Roman basilicas did not face the entrance—that is, the East—during the Offertory prayer—i.e., that they really faced the altar—this still would not have meant that the priest and the faithful faced one another, because during the Eucharistic Prayer the altar was hidden behind curtains. As St. John Chrysostom

---

108 See Tertullian, *Adv. Val.* (PL 2:515): *Nostrae columbae etiam domus simplex, in editis semper et apertis et ad lucem* ("Even the house of our Dove is simple, always on places high and open, and facing the light"); see also St. Beissel, *Bilder aus der Geschichte der altchristlichen Kunst und Liturgie in Italien (Images from the History of Ancient Christian Art and Liturgy in Italy)*, Freiburg, 1899, p. 84; see also J. Dölger, *Sol salutis*, p. 121.

109 See St. Beissel, *Bilder aus der Geschichte der altchristlichen Kunst und Liturgie in Italien (Images from the History of Ancient Christian Art and Liturgy in Italy)*, p. 265.

has reported, the curtains would be lifted again only after the litany had been sung by the deacon.[110]

Thus, the faithful worshiping in the basilicas in which the entrance and not the apse were situated at the East end, did not face the altar in prayer. Neither, however, did they have their backs turned towards the altar, which would have been an impossible thing to do considering their ancient belief that the altar is sacred. Since the faithful were situated in the side naves, they had the altar at their left or at their right, thus forming a semi-circle open towards the East, with the celebrant and his assistants being positioned at its vertex.[111]

How does all this relate to church buildings in which the apse is situated at the East end of the building? That would depend on the particular position taken up by the faithful. If they were assembled in a wide semi-circle, open towards the apse where the altar was located, then we still have an orientation towards the East, but with the liturgy now placed in the center, not at the vertex. Here the altar is placed in a position which, in fact, sets it farther apart from the faithful.

During the Middle Ages, the faithful were almost always situated in the center nave, with the side naves having become the venues used for processions. This pattern of the

110 See Fr. van de Paverd, "Zur Geschichte der Messliturgie in Antiocheia und Konstantinopel gegen Ende des 4. Jh." ("About the History of the Liturgy of the Mass in Antioch and Constantinople Towards the End of the Fourth Century"), *Orientalia Christiana Analecta*, Vol. 187, Rome, 1970, pp. 42ff., 187 ff.; see also my review of this work, *Byzantinische Zeitschrift*, Vol. 65, 1972, pp. 371ff.

111 See L. Bouyer, *Mensch und Ritus (Man and the Rite)*, 1964, p. 213: "The idea that the basilica is the ideal shape for a Christian church building, because it facilitates a celebration during which the priest and the faithful are facing one another, is complete nonsense. Indeed, this viewpoint would have been the last thing the early Christians would have thought of."

faithful formed behind the priest-celebrant added a new, dynamic and directional dimension; it was like the procession of the People of God into the Promised Land. Facing the East was to indicate the direction and destination of this procession: the lost paradise to be found in the East (Gen. 2:8). The celebrant and his assistants formed the vanguard of the procession to the East.[112] When compared to the dynamic, directional nature of the faithful in procession, the earlier formation of the faithful assembled for prayer in an open semi-circle expressed a stationary principle: the waiting for the Lord who, having ascended to the East (Ps. 67:34), will come again from the East (Acts 1:11), the open semi-circle representing the natural state of waiting and expectation. When we expect the arrival of an important person, the group of waiting people will form into the shape of a semi-circle to receive the expected person into their midst.

St. John of Damascus, in his work, *De fide orthodoxa*, IV, 12, expresses a similar thought when he says,

> When ascending into heaven, He rose towards the East, and that is how the Apostles adored Him, and He will return just as they saw Him ascend into heaven, as the Lord has said: "Just as the flash of lightening rises from above and then descends downward, so will be the arrival of the Lord." Waiting for Him, we adore Him facing East. This is an unrecorded tradition passed down to us from the Apostles.[113]

112 Similar ideas can be found in R. Schwarz, *Vom Bau der Kirche* (*On the Building of Churches*), Würzburg, 1938, pp. 126ff.

113 Quoted according to J. Dölger (see Footnote 90), *Sol salutis*, p. 176ff.

As Nussbaum correctly observes, modern man no longer understands the significance and meaning of the act of facing East in prayer.[114] For modern man, the sun no longer carries the symbolic significance it did for the man of antiquity. But that observation does not really apply when we consider the practice of the priest and the faithful facing in the same direction in prayer.

St. Augustine's call that we mentioned before—that the faithful should *conversi ad Dominum*—is timeless, and meaningful even in our time. It is also, as Kunstmann observes, a way of "looking for the Lord's place."[115] We now turn to examine the sociological aspect of the celebration *versus populum*. The professor of sociology W. Siebel, in his work, *Liturgie als Angebot*[116] (*Liturgy On Offer*), expresses his belief that the priest facing the people "represents the best and primary symbol of the new spirit in liturgy." He continues,

...the practice (of the priest facing the other way) that had been in use before gave the impression that the priest was the leader and representative of the faithful acting as a spokesperson for the faithful, like Moses on Mount Sinai. The faithful assumed the role of sending a message (prayer, adoration, sacrifice); the priest functioned as the

114 See O. Nussbaum, "Zelebration *versus populum* und Opfercharakter der Messe" ("Celebration *versus populum* and the Character of the Mass as a Sacrifice"), *Zeitschrift für katholische Theologie*, Vol. 93, 1971, pp. 148ff., pp. 163ff.

115 See J. Kunstmann, "Ort des Herrn"("The Place of the Lord"), *Priesterjahrheft 1971*, Paderborn, 1971, pp. 33ff.

116 See W. Siebel, *Liturgie als Angebot. Bemerkungen aus soziologischer Sicht* (*Liturgy On Offer: Comments on the Sociological Aspect*), Morus Press, Berlin, 1972, pp. 16ff.: "Wendung zum Volk" ("Facing the People").

leader delivering the message; God as the recipient of the message.

In his new role, continues Siebel, the priest

hardly continues to function as the representative of the faithful, but as an actor who plays God's role, at least during the central part of the Mass, similar to what is played out in *Oberammergau* and other religious plays.

Siebel draws this conclusion:

This new turn of events having changed the priest into an actor expected to play the role of Christ on stage, in the re-enactment of the Last Supper, makes the persons of Christ and the priest merge in a way that heretofore had been impermissible.

Siebel explains the readiness with which almost all priests accepted the *versus populum* celebration:

The considerable level of insecurity and loneliness experienced by the priest naturally brings about a search for new emotional support structures. A part of this emotional support is the support provided by the faithful. Yet, this support also leads to a new form of dependency: the dependency of the actor on his audience.

In his article, "Pubertätserscheinungen in der Katholischen Kirche" ("Signs of Puberty in the Catholic Church"), K. G. Rey observes in a similar way,

While in the past, the priest functioned as the anonymous go-between, the first among the faithful, facing God and not the people, representative of all and together with them offering the Sacrifice, while reciting prayers that have been prescribed for him—today he is a distinct person, with personal characteristics, his personal life-style, his face turned towards the people. For many priests this change is a temptation they cannot handle, the prostitution of their person. Some priests are quite adept—some less so—at taking personal advantage of a situation. Their gestures, their facial expressions, their movements, their overall behavior, all serve to subjectively attract attention to their person. Some draw attention to themselves by making repetitive observations, issuing instructions, and lately, by delivering personalized addresses of welcome and farewell...To them, the level of success in their performance is a measure of their personal power and thus the indicator of their feeling of personal security and self-assurance.[117]

The view advanced by Klauser, cited above, that the celebration *versus populum* "serves to more clearly express the eucharistic community around the table," is addressed by Siebel in his work, *Liturgy on Offer*:[118]

The intended pulling closer together of the people around the table of the Lord's Supper hardly contributes to a strengthening of the sense of community. It is only the priest who is actually at the table, and *standing* at the

117 See K. G. Rey, "Pubertätserscheinungen in der katholischen Kirche" ("Signs of Puberty in the Catholic Church"), *Kritische Texte*, Benzinger, Vol. 4, p. 25.

118 See W. Siebel, *Liturgie als Angebot. Bemerkungen aus soziologischer Sicht* (*Liturgy on Offer: Comments on the Sociological Aspect*), p. 18.

table, at that. The other partakers in the supper are sitting, closer or farther removed, in the auditorium.

To this, Siebel adds another observation:

> Usually, the altar table is situated at a distance and it is elevated, which means that the sense of togetherness that existed in the room where the Last Supper took place simply cannot be re-created. Facing the people, it is difficult for the priest not to give the impression that he is trying very hard to sell us something. To correct this impression, attempts are made to move the altar into the midst of the faithful. In that way, the individual does not have to look just at the priest, he can now also look at the person next to him or at the person sitting across from him. Moving the altar into the midst of the faithful, however, also means that the space between a sacral center and the faithful is being lost. The holy fear that used to seize us when entering the church where God was really present, is replaced by weak sentiment, a response to something that is little more than ordinary.

From a sociological perspective, placing the priest behind the altar, facing the people, turns him into an actor, totally dependent on his audience, and also into a salesman offering his wares to the public. And if he has any talent at all, he can develop into a real huckster.

The reading of the Gospel, on the other hand, is something entirely different. It requires that the priest face the people. Accordingly, in the old basilicas, with the entrance being placed at the East side, the faithful faced the apse (West) during the Liturgy of the Word. In this situation, when proclaiming the Gospel, the priest is, indeed, making an offer to the public. Just as there is no question that the priest face the people during the homily, the lector or reader should read the Gospel facing the people—which, incidentally, was not always the case, presumably due to a sense of reverence for the Word of God.

Something entirely different again, as we have already observed, is the actual Liturgy of the Eucharist. Here, the liturgy is no longer just an "offer" to the people but a holy event, an event when heaven and earth unite and God's grace flows to us. Here, the direction of the participant and that of the priest must be focused in prayer on the Lord. It is only during the Communion of the Faithful, which is the Eucharistic meal in its true sense, that we again have the priest facing the individual communicant.

This alternating change in the position of the priest at the altar during the celebration of the Mass carries an important symbolic and sociological meaning. During prayer and sac-rifice, the priest, together with the people, faces God, just as he faces the people when he proclaims the Word of God and gives Communion. Until now, this basic concept has always been accepted, in East and West, in the early Church and during the Baroque period. It is only quite recently that the Roman Church has undertaken a change, a change that, for one thing, rests on a wrong view of history, but is based primarily on theological considerations. The future will tell what the consequences of this change are going to be.

VIII

Attempting to Resolve the Problem

Bearing all this in mind, we now have to look for a solution to the liturgical problem. At this particular point, these are the options:

The traditional *ritus Romanus* and the *ritus modernus* should both be accepted as legitimate forms of liturgical worship. The two rites are to exist as independent rites and must be kept separate and unique in such a way that the traditional Roman rite and the traditionally used *Missale Romanum*, together with all other liturgical texts (*Rituale* and *Pontificale*), be reinstated or be authorized for use in the form in which they existed prior to the Council. The changes made in the liturgy following the conclusion of the Council should apply only to the *ritus modernus*. This would include, among other things, the change in the words of Consecration, which evoked such a sense of scandal among many priests, as well as the new Eucharistic Prayers and the new Order of Readings, which because of its many shortcomings should be promptly replaced by a better one.

The currently valid form of the Mass would then no longer be considered as the Roman rite, but as a unique rite, *ad experimentum*. Only the future will tell whether or not this new rite would be commonly accepted and is here to stay. It is reasonable to assume that the new liturgical texts will not be in use much longer, for the simple reason that the progressive forces in the Church will certainly continue to develop, or have already developed, new ideas about how to "design" the liturgy of the Mass.

However, this parallel existence of two rites would present difficulties, because of the changes made to the liturgical calendar, i.e., the new Sunday calendar, and the Sanctoral, assigning the feasts of Saints on Sundays. But these difficulties can be overcome.

Since there is no basis for it in liturgical history, nor in theology, nor sociologically, the celebration of the Mass *versus populum* should be gradually phased out.

Concerning the *ritus Romanus*, as intended by the Second Vatican Council, we should consider enriching the traditional liturgy by including a greater number of Prefaces to be drawn from the treasure of the ancient Roman *Sacramentarium*, as well as extending the order of readings to include more scriptural readings. However, these additions to the traditional order of the Mass should, for the time being, be *ad libitum*, i.e., be left to the personal preference of the priest-celebrant. To emphasize more strongly the liturgical year, the feasts of "minor" Saints could be celebrated only in a *Memoria* format. It would also go without saying that even in the *ritus Romanus*, the scriptural readings would use the vernacular.

There is nothing to be gained in applying the current experiments—and that is what most of the changes are—to the traditional Roman rite as, unfortunately, has been done. To do this destroys an important element: the continuity of liturgical forms of worship, a subject repeatedly raised in these pages. If we allow the traditional rite to continue unchanged and nurture it, alongside the new rite but allowing the traditional rite to exist as a living liturgy, not as a museum piece, it will manifest itself within the universe of the Church and among the different peoples as an important element: the unity of cult.

In a similar way, the traditional *ritus Romanus*, which is more "modern" than many would like to believe, by its use of Latin, a common language which during the Middle Ages served to unite the peoples of Europe, can help in bringing today's people closer together in worship, instead of separating them along language barriers.

This, of course, was a wish of the Second Vatican Council overlooked in the ensuing pandemonium of liturgical reform. Especially in geographical areas with mixed ethnic populations, for example in the Southern Tyrol, the Latin liturgy would be a blessing.

Many problems in today's Church would be resolved by the strict separation of the Roman rite and the new vernacular liturgy, the *ritus modernus*, and by making both forms of liturgy available to the people, as we have recommended.

Above all, this would reduce the peril of a larger schism by meeting the justified demands of countless Catholics—up to half of those who are still practicing their faith—to be able to attend Mass according to the traditional rite, without ignoring the demands of those who prefer a "contemporary" liturgy.

All this, of course, has happened before! Levitin-Krasnov tells us about a similar attempt at reform in the Russian Orthodox Church during the years following the October Revolution. At that time, different attempts were made to no longer celebrate Mass within the *sanctum* of the altar room, but instead in the center of the church. The liturgy was translated into modern Russian and prayers were supplemented by using parts from other liturgies. The private prayers of the priest were recited publicly so that the faithful could hear them. The singing of church hymns by the faithful was introduced to replace the traditional chants sung by the choir, and so on and so forth.[119]

This liturgical crisis in Russia has now passed and the traditional forms of liturgy have been restored. In spite of (or because of?) this "outmoded" liturgy, which, as we know, remains the only way for the Church to "propagandize" herself, spiritual life has entered a stage of bloom, which is more than what we can say about our situation in the West.

During the Age of Enlightenment, when there were attempts at reform in the Church similar to what we are witnessing today, the Bishop of Regensburg, Michael Sailer, who died in 1832, wrote these words of warning:

> When using your right hand to hold on strongly to the old, which is tried and true, and your left hand to introduce that which is new and better, then give your heart to the one eternal truth that constantly rejuvenates itself in the old and does not deny its old glory in the new...Whoever wants to reform the liturgy must begin by nurturing inspired, blessed priests.

Bishop Sailer continues:

> It would also appear that many an advocate for the rapid introduction of the German language (into the liturgy) was lacking in common sense, otherwise his better judgment would have been: Don't expect too much from the German word...The Protestant Churches, with all their new hymnals and liturgical innovations, are emptying. This may very well happen to us, as well. I am afraid that we are driving away those who have been attending our

119 See Levitin-Krasnov, *Böse Jahre (Bad Years)*, p. 175.

worship services all along, without gaining much in those whom we seek to attract.[120]

One common argument advanced against the solution we have presented here is that the parallel existence of two rites would undermine the concept of Church unity at the individual parish level.

To this we can respond that in the universal Church there have always been a number of different rites, particularly in the Eastern Church, which are duly recognized by the Church. Therefore, it cannot be that serious a matter to have two distinct rites co-existing in the Roman Church, at least for a little while. Indeed, if only we had just two rites to contend with in today's Church! As we all know, we now have an abundance of individual "rites," since so many priests now design their own liturgy, just as they please.

In this environment, can we really talk about a unity of the liturgical rite?

Today, we are standing before the ruins of almost 2,000 years of Church tradition. We cannot help being apprehensive: the numerous reforms made have damaged Church tradition to such an extent that it will be difficult to bring it back again. Today, dare we even ask whether after such a deconstruction, a reconstruction of the traditional Order would be possible? But one must not give up hope.

120 See J. M. Sailer, "Neue Beiträge zur Bildung des Geistlichen" ("New Remarks Concerning the Formation of Clerics"), *Sämtliche Werke*, Vol. 19, Sulzbach, 1839, pp. 277ff.

IX

The Destruction of the Roman Rite

The quarrel about the "new Mass" continues unabated and the opposing front lines are growing more and more rigid. While some reject the new rite as heretical, even as invalid, others see it as the long awaited breakthrough for new forms of liturgy and the opportunity actually to live as an ecclesial community.

The following discussion addresses the question of whether the new Mass merely represents the implementation of a "renewed liturgy," as envisioned by the Second Vatican Council—a liturgy not significantly different from the traditional one—or whether the new Mass is, indeed, a new rite, in its spirit as well as its form.

There are many priests and faithful who deliberately oppose the new liturgy. Since they cling to the traditional liturgical forms, we now have a situation where, to use a phrase frequently quoted from the *Announcement of the German Conference of Bishops*, "Altar stands against altar."

At one of these altars, "traditionalists" disappointed with and alienated from the post-conciliar Church continue to celebrate what they call the unchanged Mass of Pope St. Pius V; while at the other altar, which for many has become but an ordinary meal table, the "progressives," as well as the

majority of those priests trained to render unquestioning
obedience to the Church hierarchy, conduct with their people a Eucharistic celebration, for which they follow, some
more so than others, the new liturgical rubrics.

The "traditionalist" priest will always stand in front of the
altar, as has been commonly done in the Eastern Church and
in the Western Church throughout history. They are priests
offering a sacrifice who, together with the faithful, face God.

The other priests function as presiders over a Eucharistic
meal; and from their seats, or from behind the altar facing the
people, which has become a table, they direct their gaze
towards the assembled faithful. They are, apparently, not
troubled in the least by the fact that their backs are turned on
the former High Altar and on the tabernacle—the altar at
which, only a few years ago, the holy sacrifice of the Mass
was offered and on which the eyes of the praying faithful had
been focused.

In the years before the reform, no Catholic could have
imagined that the Roman Church, founded on the Rock of
Peter, would undergo such changes and at the same time
cause such confusion among its members.

Of course, it is true that there have been progressives,
particularly during the Age of Enlightenment, who, in part
because of erroneous interpretations of history, in part because of "modern" theological views, pressed for changes in
the liturgy as it was then practiced. In the past, the Church's
teaching Magisterium has carefully guarded against such
developments and has always been able to control the emer-
gence of radical ideas.

Now, all this has fundamentally changed. Today, those
who out of a sense of personal belief hold firm to what until
recently had been strictly prescribed by the Roman Church
are treated with condescension by many of their own brothers. They face problems if they continue to nurture the very
rite in which they were brought up and to which they have

been consecrated. That theirs were decisions made as a matter of conscience and that their conscience is being sorely tested is of little consequence to those who oppose them.

On the other side, the progressives who see little or no value in tradition can do almost no wrong, and are usually given the benefit of the doubt, even when they defend opinions which clearly contradict Catholic teaching.

To add to this spiritual confusion, we are also dealing with the satiated state of mind of modern man who, living in our consumer society, approaches anything that is holy with a complete lack of understanding and has no appreciation of the concept of religion, let alone of his own sinful state. For them, God, if they believe in Him at all, exists only as their "friend."

At this critical juncture, the traditional Roman rite, more than one thousand years old and until now the heart of the Church, was destroyed. A closer examination reveals that the Roman rite was not perfect, and that some elements of value had atrophied over the centuries. Yet, through all the periods of unrest that again and again shook the Church to her foundations, the Roman rite always remained the rock, the secure home of faith and piety.

Instead of fabricating a new liturgy by committee, it would have sufficed to bring back some of what had been lost in the past, thus making the liturgy more vigorous and relevant, as the Council Fathers had expressed in the *Constitution on the Sacred Liturgy*.

The document makes no mention of the traditional rite being abolished; it mentions only the concern about the pastoral care of the faithful, which should be assigned greater importance through such means as, for example, making greater use of the vernacular or introducing additional readings to enrich the Missal.

But what possible advantage can be gained for the pastoral care of the faithful by changing the feast days of the saints in the Church calendar, changing the way of counting Sundays during the liturgical year, or even changing the words of Consecration? What possible advantage can be gained by introducing a completely new Order of Readings and abolishing the old one, or by making minor and unimportant adjustments to the traditional rite, and then finally, by publishing a new Missal?

Was all this really done because of a pastoral concern about the souls of the faithful, or did it not rather represent a radical breach with the traditional rite, to prevent the further use of traditional liturgical texts and thus to make the celebration of the "Tridentine Mass" impossible—because it no longer reflected the new spirit moving through the Church?

Indeed, it should come as no surprise to anyone that the prohibition of the traditional rite was announced at the same time as the introduction of the new liturgical texts; and that a dispensation to continue celebrating the Mass according to the traditional rite was granted only to older priests.

Obviously, the reformers wanted a completely new liturgy, a liturgy that differed from the traditional one in spirit as well as in form; and in no way a liturgy that represented what the Council Fathers had envisioned, i.e., a liturgy that would meet the pastoral needs of the faithful.

Liturgy and faith are interdependent. That is why a new rite was created, a rite that in many ways reflects the bias of the new (modernist) theology. The traditional liturgy simply could not be allowed to exist in its established form because it was permeated with the truths of the traditional faith and the ancient forms of piety. For this reason alone, much was abolished and new rites, prayers and hymns were introduced, as were the new readings from Scripture, which conveniently left out those passages that did not square with the teachings of modern theology—for example, references to a God who judges and punishes.

At the same time, the priests and the faithful are told that the new liturgy created after the Second Vatican Council is identical in essence with the liturgy that has been in use in the Catholic Church up to this point, and that the only changes introduced involved reviving some earlier liturgical forms and removing a few duplications, but above all getting rid of elements of no particular interest.

Most priests accepted these assurances about the continuity of liturgical forms of worship and accepted the new rite with the same unquestioning obedience with which they had accepted the minor ritual changes introduced by Rome from time to time in the past, changes beginning with the reform of the Divine Office and of the liturgical chant introduced by Pope St. Pius X.

Following this strategy, the groups pushing for reform were able to take advantage of and at the same time abuse the sense of obedience among the older priests, and the common good will of the majority of the faithful, while, in many cases, they themselves refused to obey.

The pastoral benefits that so many idealists had hoped the new liturgy would bring did not materialize. Our churches emptied in spite of the new liturgy (or because of it?), and the faithful continue to fall away from the Church in droves.

Although our young people have been literally seduced into supporting the new forms of liturgical worship, they have, in fact, become more and more alienated from the faith. They are drawn to religious sects—Christian and non-Christian ones— because fewer and fewer priests teach them the riches of our Catholic faith and the tenets of Christian morality. As for older people, the radical changes made to the traditional liturgy have taken from them the sense of security in their religious home.

Today, many among us wonder: Is this the Spring people had hoped would emerge from the Second Vatican Council? Instead of a genuine renewal in our Church, we have seen only novelties. Instead of our religious life entering a period of new invigoration, as has happened in the past, what we see now is a form of Christianity that has turned towards the world.

We are now involved in a liturgy in which God is no longer the center of our attention. Today, the eyes of our faithful are no longer focused on God's Son having become Man hanging before us on the cross, or on the pictures of His saints, but on the human community assembled for a commemorative meal. The assembly of people is sitting there, face to face with the "presider," expecting from him, in accordance with the "modern" spirit of the Church, not so much a transfer of God's grace, but primarily some good ideas and advice on how to deal with daily life and its challenges.

There are few people left who speak of the Holy Mass as the Sacrifice of the New Covenant which we offer to God the Father through Jesus Christ, or of the sacramental union with Christ that we experience when we receive Holy Communion. Today, we are dealing with the "Eucharistic feast," and with the "holy bread" to be shared among us as a sign of our brotherhood with Jesus.

The real destruction of the traditional Mass, of the traditional Roman rite with a history of more than one thousand years, is the wholesale destruction of the faith on which it was based, a faith that had been the source of our piety and of our courage to bear witness to Christ and His Church, the inspiration of countless Catholics over many centuries. Will someone, some day, be able to say the same thing about the new Mass?

Many loyal Catholics agonize over the question: what can be done about the loss of our faith and the destruction of our liturgy?

We can be certain that it is probably impossible—and maybe not even desirable—to return the Church to exactly the same state in which it existed after the Second World War. It would be a realistic solution to accept the *Constitution on the Sacred Liturgy* of the Second Vatican Council in the way in which the majority of the Council Fathers had intended it to be implemented: as a reform of the traditional Roman rite within prescribed limits, with the *proviso* that the rite as such must not be destroyed.

To bring this about would, of course, require that those in positions of power and influence in our Church return to "sound teaching" (2 Tim. 4:3), and so should all our professors of theology. It is essential to again understand the celebration of the Holy Mass primarily as liturgical worship, a solemn cult, with God, not man, at its center.

We must thank God that there are still a large number of priests and faithful who have not been infected by the new teachings and who continue to survive on the substance of the faith received from past centuries. We are fortunate to still have priests who continue to be resourceful and pious, toiling for the Kingdom of God. They have accepted the new liturgical texts in the churches strictly out of a sense of obedience to the Holy Father, and as many others have done, they too have set up an altar facing the people, fearing that if they did not do so, their people would say that they were behind the times.

X

Liturgy, Our Home
The Need for an Unchanging Liturgy

Deep in the heart of every person there is the longing for home, and we can only experience the real meaning of home when we are away from it.

The word *Heimat* (home or fatherland) is a uniquely German concept. Exactly what meaning does it convey? *Heimat* is the environment known to us since childhood, the house in which we grew up, the natural surroundings with their people and their habits and customs. To us, the *heimat* is always beautiful, even if others don't share our feelings for it.

Man's longing for home is his longing for what is familiar and known. It also is a longing for security based on the familiarity of a person's surroundings. Finally, it is the sense of security that the small child feels when he is with his mother and that he misses as an adult when faced with the uncertainties of life.

The religious person seeks security in the Church as his Mother. In her he hopes to find shelter and help for his troubled soul, answers to the probing questions posed by his intellect, but above all, he wants certainty about the Last

Things. What he seeks is the Church as an oasis of tranquility and peace, peace "such as the world cannot give" (Jn. 14:27).

In the past, a person was able to find safety and shelter in the Church, even though she had many imperfections. His questions were always answered in a certain and precise way, even if he did not always find that the answers he received satisfied him completely. Today, instead of a clear answer, he will receive a description of the problem, a response that does not do very much to help him find inner peace.

Last, but certainly not least, the religious person seeks home and shelter in the celebration of liturgical worship, in the rites and feasts known to him since childhood: these are intimately connected to his faith. For him, the unchanging cult is a part of his *Heimat*.

These observations apply equally to non-Christian religions. Missionaries come across these concepts all the time. When they bring individual members of a tribe to accept Christianity, they also tear them out of the social structure of their tribes, with all their rituals, customs and traditions. It usually takes some time until the newly converted adapt to their new home, the Christian cult: the old rituals of their tribe continue to pull them back with the force of a strong magnet.

A people that decides to relinquish its traditional rites is in acute danger of relinquishing its own existence as a people. Kurt Ziesel says that much in his book, *Die Sensation des Guten* (*The Sensation of the Good*, Würzburg, 1966), when he writes about the "destruction of the idea of the [Japanese] Emperor as God, and with it, the destruction of Shintoism as the state religion." He says that

> together with the destruction of the cult of the Emperor came the destruction of the world of the samurai and of ancestor worship—all integral parts of the Shinto con-

cept and with its destruction, Japan lost its very soul. The roots that connected the Japanese people with their spiritual and religious foundation were severed, and nothing was put in its place.

A Catholic who ceased to be an active member of the Church for the past generation and who, having decided to return to the Church, wants to become religiously active again, probably would not recognize today's Church as the one he had left. Simply by entering a Catholic church, particularly if it happens to be one of ultra-modern design, he will feel as if he had entered a strange, foreign place. He will think that he must have come to the wrong address and that he has accidentally ended up in some other Christian religious community.

The accustomed pictures and statues in the church have disappeared. Instead of a cross hanging over the altar there now is some often undefinable "work of art"; the altar itself being a bare slab of rock, akin to a barrow. In vain will he look for the tabernacle on the altar; nor will he find the communion rail. He will miss the smell of incense that he remembers to have always lingered after Mass. He may not even find a confessional.

The Catholic woman who many years ago became reconciled to the faith of her Protestant husband will have a similar experience. She continued to go to a Catholic church to attend Mass because that is where she felt at home. Would she feel the same way today, when there seems hardly a difference between a Catholic and a Protestant worship service?

The reformers of our liturgy have failed to consider adequately and address the issue of how the traditional forms of liturgical worship, even if they were not entirely satisfactory, nevertheless inspired among the faithful a sense of belonging, of feeling at home. They also failed to consider and deal with the issue of the extent to which simply abolishing these forms of liturgy would also result in a loss of faith among the people, particularly among the less educated. The reformers also failed to understand the significance of many of the ethnic elements that were a part of the liturgy.

For example, for many among the faithful the traditional, solemn *Rorate* Mass celebrated during Advent was an important part of their religious home; and this was also true for Requiem Masses and funeral rites. The Solemn Requiem Mass according to the traditional form, which appealed directly to the heart, has almost completely disappeared. Yet here especially, great care should have been taken in introducing changes, because the customs associated with burial rites are the ones to which people in any cultural setting are most strongly attached.

Language is a part of "home" also. A person returning from a trip abroad and suddenly hearing the familiar local dialect, knows that he is now home again.

In the same way, a particular language is associated with the cult. That language can never be the language commonly used in everyday conversation. All highly developed religions have their own language of cult. In Islam, Old Arabic is used, even in the non-Arab speaking areas of Asia and Africa. The Jews conduct their prayer services in the synagogue in Old Hebrew.

Until today, the language used in the Roman Church was Latin, which, so we were told, served as a common bond among the different people of the world. Today, the use of Latin in liturgical worship has been almost entirely eliminated, which, if we may point this out, is clearly in violation of the instructions issued by the Liturgical Commission (see Article 54).

This is not the place to develop the problematic issue of cult language. What we can say is that for pastoral reasons, some parts of the liturgy should be said in the vernacular, particularly the readings, the general intercessions, and parts of the liturgy of the Communion of the Faithful. At the same time, we must not overlook the fact that more than ever in our time it is important that liturgical worship serve as a unifying factor, with millions of people now routinely travelling in foreign countries.

The liturgy continues to be our home even if it develops and changes over time. During the course of the almost 2,000 years of Church history it has evolved constantly. But the important point to consider here is that in the past there has never been an actual break with Church tradition, as has happened now, and in such a frightening way, where almost everything the Church represents is being questioned.

It is true that the historical development of our liturgy has not always proceeded evenly and that it has not always had happy results. Wrong decisions were made on a number of occasions; had they not been made, the traditional forms most likely would not have been challenged.

It will be some time until we will be in a position to measure fully the pastoral damage caused to the faithful by the reforms, which were not just imprudent and hurried, but above all did not evolve in a normal, organic way. We must expect that sooner or later we will be facing almost empty pews in our churches, as the Protestant Reformed Churches have been experiencing for decades now, while, we may point out, that has not been the case in the Lutheran Church which has maintained many of its traditional forms of liturgy. In the end, we will all have to recognize that the new liturgical forms, well-intentioned as they may have been at the beginning, did not provide the people with bread, but with stones.

To summarize what we have said: there is nothing wrong with the liturgy developing in an organic fashion, and there most certainly is nothing wrong with promptly removing from it any redundancies or any elements that no longer meet the needs of our time! But this development has to move in a prudent way, duly considering the real pastoral care of the faithful, so that they are not left with the impression that everything traditional has been wrong and in error, and certainly without taking from them the liturgy that they thought to be their Home.

And we must not forget that liturgical forms, if they are to endure, always grow from a living and steady faith. Yet, it is precisely this faith that is largely lacking among us. In this sense, it would also appear to be futile to renew the faith through a renewed liturgy, for example, to renew our faith in the Resurrection of our Lord by designing a new liturgy for Easter night.

Faith is a precondition of liturgy. The teaching of our faith is first and foremost a pastoral function, and as such should be as relevant and "modern" as it can be. But this teaching function can only be accomplished to a limited extent during the celebration of the liturgy: teaching has to precede liturgy.

Yet, in many cases, the introduction of changes that in themselves may be well intentioned and useful will have the opposite result, for the simple reason that "the people" don't care for them.

Particularly pernicious in this respect is the incessant nature of the changes to which we are subjected. This is diametrically opposed to the concept of liturgy as our home. To constantly change a ritual and to abolish almost completely time-honored customs and traditions is synonymous with robbing a person of his religious home and thus shaking the foundations of his faith. The new assignment of the feasts of saints in the Church calendar published at the very outset of the liturgical reforms, a completely unnecessary and radical change, only served to alienate the faithful. Even a person who has but a superficial knowledge of how the psychology of a people works is bound to agree with these observations.

Frequently overlooked is the close association between Catholic teaching and certain forms of piety, an association in which the average Catholic person places stock. To many Catholics, a change in liturgical forms also means a change in the faith to which they have been attached.

It is easy to abolish something, but it is quite difficult to put something better in its place. Once an old order that has been the religious home for most people has been destroyed, it will take a long, long time to build a new one.

XI

Concluding Remarks

Great is the confusion! Who can still see clearly in this darkness? Where in our Church are the leaders who can show us the right path? Where are the bishops courageous enough to cut out the cancerous growth of modernist theology that has implanted itself and is festering within the celebration of even the most sacred mysteries, before the cancer spreads and causes even greater damage?

What we need today is a new Athanasius, a new Basil, bishops like those who in the fourth century courageously fought against Arianism when almost the whole of Christendom had succumbed to the heresy. We need saints today who can unite those whose faith has remained firm so that we might fight error and rouse the weak and vacillating from their apathy.

We cannot and must not leave the fight for the preservation and re-establishment of the traditional liturgy of the Mass to a small group of fanatics who reject outright even those liturgical reforms demanded by the last Council, reforms which are justified, such as the use of the local vernacular in some situations.

We can only pray and hope that the Roman Church will return to Tradition and allow once more the celebration of that liturgy of the Mass which is well over 1,000 years old. Why should it not be possible to have two rites, the traditional and the new rite, coexisting peacefully, just as in the East where there are many different rites and liturgies, or even in the West where there still exist particular rites, such as the rite of Milan? And in any case, if the new rite is to be continued, it must be improved.

We are living in a time when there is little faith left. The call grows louder and louder to save what we can. As strange as this may sound, the truly "modern" forces in our Church today are not the so-called "Progressives," who want to abandon customs developed over time and replace them with experiments of uncertain value, but rather the "conservatives" who recognize the value of Church tradition and are sensitive to pastoral needs.

In the final analysis, this means that in the future the traditional rite of the Mass must be retained in the Roman Catholic Church, and not only as a means to accommodate older priests and lay people, but as the primary liturgical form for the celebration of Mass. It must become once more the norm of our faith and the symbol of Catholic unity throughout the world, a rock of stability in a period of upheaval and never-ending change.

Part II

Facing the Lord

On the Building of Churches
and Facing East in Prayer

XII

Author's Introduction

*Our altar is one from which the priests of the
sacred tent have no right to eat.* (Heb. 13:10)

An altar is always associated with a sacrifice being offered
by a priest. The altar, the priest and the sacrifice are interre-
lated, as St. John Chrysostom observed, "Nobody can be a
priest without the sacrifice" (PG 63:111). In a strict sense, we
can say that since the Protestant Christians purposely reject
the sacrifice of the Mass and the priesthood, they really have
no need for an altar.

In all the ancient religions, the priest, while offering the
sacrifice, stands removed from the people (see Heb. 5:1),
before the altar, in front of the Holy of Holies, the image of
the Deity. During the sacrificial meal, the participants in the
sacrifice go up to the altar to receive a share of the altar from
the priest who has offered the sacrifice. As St. Paul writes,
"Are not those who eat the sacrificial meal partners in the
altar?" (1 Cor. 10:18).

During the past twenty years, we have experienced a
change in the accepted meaning of the Sacrifice. Personally,
I believe that the introduction of the "Altar of the People,"
with the Mass celebrant facing the people, is of much greater

significance and poses greater problems for the future than the introduction of the new Missal. This is so because the new position taken by the priest at the altar—which is without any doubt an innovation and not a return to a practice of the early Church—is based upon a new conception of the Mass: that of the "eucharistic community around the table."

The predominant concept of the Mass until this present period, that of worshipping and adoring God, together with the sacrificial character of the celebration considered as the mystical representation and actualization of the death and Resurrection of Our Lord, has now been relegated to a secondary level. Similarly, the relationship between Christ's Sacrifice and our offering of bread and wine is scarcely apparent. This question is examined in detail in my study, Das Opfer der Kirche (*The Church's Sacrifice*).

I am not one of those who maintain that the shape and design of the altar as it developed over the centuries, and was maintained until the Second Vatican Council, should never be changed. On the contrary, I prefer a return to the simple design that existed throughout the Eastern and Western Church during the first millennium—and still exists in the Eastern Church to this day—a design that manifests the function of the Christian altar as the location for the Sacrifice of the New Testament.

Last year, reading a continuing series of letters published in the *Deutsche Tagespost*, it occurred to me that there is a need for detailed commentary on the problem presented by the modern altar facing the people and by the celebrant facing the people—a commentary written with the general reader in mind. These letters revealed that there continues to be much confusion about the historical development of the altar and that there are a number of commonly accepted but erroneous ideas about the early Church that go unchallenged. In view of this, I have purposely sought to address the very concerns reflected in the letters to the editor of the *Deutsche Tagespost*.

In the *Addendum* to this book, I again deal with the controversial translation of the text passage "for you and for all" used in the consecration formula. My observations about this incorrect translation are not limited to its philological and soteriological aspects, as many comments are these days, but rather, extend to the understanding of the Mass as a sacrifice. For some readers, the theological arguments I am presenting will be quite new.

Klaus Gamber
Pentecost, 1987

XIII

The Altar and the Sanctuary: Then and Now

With such longing I see you in the sanctuary and behold your power and glory. (Ps. 62:3)

And I shall be satisfied when your glory shall appear. (Ps. 16:15)

The words of the Psalmist give us an insight into the state of mind of the faithful in the Old Testament when they entered the Temple in Jerusalem; the Psalm asks nothing less than what Moses asked of God—to be allowed to behold His countenance (Ex. 32:11-23). But just as Moses was only able to see the "back of Yahweh," so the faithful Israelite saw only God's sanctuary; and even if he was a member of the caste of priests, he would only get to see the exterior of that sanctuary.

The visitor to the Christian house of God (*domus Dei*) should enter it with the same purpose in mind as did the Psalmist: to behold God's "glory" and to sense his "power," which is revealed to him in the liturgical rite of the Mass, in representative form. We behold the Lord in the veiled image

121

of the Eucharist, because here on earth we cannot behold God's countenance without suffering death (Ex. 32:23).

Origen reminds us that "the assemblies of the faithful are joined by the hosts of angels, as well as by the 'power' of our own Lord and Savior, and also by the spirits of the Saints" (*De orat.*, 31:5). And the Syrian poet Balaeus has this to say:

> So that we may find Him (the Lord) on earth, he builds his house among the mortals and raises altars...so that the Church may maintain life through these altars. Make no mistake about it, this is where the King abides! Let us go to the temple to behold him (BKV 64).

Over the centuries, men have built churches and cathedrals and furnished and decorated them according to their ability so that they could behold something of God's power and glory and experience it during worship. While they themselves often lived in simple dwellings, they made every sacrifice so that the house of God was magnificent: because it was *their own* sanctuary, it belonged to all of them.

Never before in history have so many churches been built as during the years immediately following the Second World War. The majority of them were utilitarian structures not designed to be works of art, yet they often cost millions to build. From a technical standpoint, they are well equipped: they have good acoustics and superb air conditioning; they are well lit and can be easily heated. The altar can be seen from all directions.

Still, they are not houses of God in the true sense: they are not a sanctuary, they are not a temple of the Lord that we can visit to adore God and ask for His grace and assistance. They are meeting facilities, places nobody wants to visit at any time other than when services are being conducted. They are designed like "apartment silos" or "people garages," as we refer to the housing complexes in our modern suburbs—

church buildings which in colloquial terms are "soul silos" or "*Pater noster* garages."

In contrast, the pilgrimage church of Ronchamp has been used as a model for all those church buildings designed and built specifically as works of art. In building this church, the well-known architect Le Corbusier, a professed agnostic, has created a true architectural work of art. *Yet, it did not turn out to be a church after all!* At best it is a place to pray, to meditate. Yet the church of Ronchamp has become a model and meeting place for subjectivist architects. This development in the design of church buildings could only result because of a growing conviction that there are no such things as "sacred spaces" that are (or should be) different from the "profane world."

The new buildings are a symbol of our time, even an indication of the dissolution of traditional norms and standards and a representation of the chaotic nature of the world in which we live. There are, however, specific laws governing the design of a place for liturgical worship, laws that are not subject to prevailing fashion and changing trends. This is where God resides, in a very special way, just as He did in the Temple of Jerusalem. This is the place where we worship God.

There is another point: what is missing here are the spiritual and theological prerequisites. Our public life has become predominantly secular in nature. Regrettably, the Christian churches have ceased to be the indispensable foundation on which Western society rests. And yet, since money does not seem to be a problem, our architects continue to build as if nothing has changed. The huge pastoral centers constructed in our suburbs give the impression that the Church is still attracting people like a large magnet.

(The future will see only simple new church buildings, relatively small in size, buildings that from the outside will not be very prominent, while their interior will be well

Fig. 1. Veliko Tirnovo (Bulgaria), Sixth Century. Sanctuary with
Choir Screen (Reconstruction). The pergola is not shown.

crafted and designed entirely for liturgical purposes. This
building style will be similar to the basilicas of early Christianity, structures which from the street level did not stand out
as buildings serving a special purpose, yet buildings with
interiors that in a splendor of curtains and lamps, but above
all through the precious decoration of the altar and sanctuary, created a suitable environment for the celebration of the
Mystery regularly taking place here.)

In more recently built churches, we encounter different
approaches on how to design the sanctuary. Unlike the de-

sign that was common during the years between the two World Wars, with several steps leading up to the altar elevating it as if it were a stage, now the altar has been made into an "altar island," moving it as close as possible to the faithful.

In the center of this altar island, we find an (often imposing) altar table (*mensa*), with no decoration. Next to it, there is the lectionary stand, made of stone just like the altar; and behind it there are three or more (upholstered) seats for the celebrant and his assistants. Then, located somewhere at the bare back wall of the church, is the tabernacle. A cross that used to be in plain view of the faithful is now mostly absent or a small one is placed directly on the altar. Also placed on the altar are, next to the usual flower arrangement, a number of candle sticks, usually grouped together, or if they are candelabra of a larger size, placed on the floor around the altar.

In comparison, the Eastern Orthodox churches still follow the same style and decorum that originated a thousand or more years ago, a style that continues to make full use of paintings and icons. Here, we are dealing with a unique and typical art form, in which the architect and the artist are bound to follow a *typos*, a traditional model—a creative process that, however, does not result in a uniform style of art and architecture.

The tradition shared by both the Eastern and Western Church held that the sanctuary, just as the inner sanctuary of the temple of Jerusalem, was to be separated from the people. Today, the concept we frequently hear proclaims that the altar should be an "altar in the middle." That concept is wrong if it refers only to a physical setting.

During Mass, the altar is the focal point of the holy event: on it lies "the Lamb with the marks of sacrifice on him," as it says in the Apocalypse (5:6). St. Hildegard of Bingen describes the altar as the "life-giving table," and goes on to say,

> When the priest...approaches the altar to celebrate the divine mysteries, there suddenly radiates from heaven a bright light. The angels descend, light surrounds the altar...and the spirits of heaven bow in reverence to the holy office (*Scivias* II, 6).

The strict separation of the sanctuary and the nave of the church came into use when the faithful began to attend worship in large numbers, that is, at the latest, shortly before the year A. D. 300. Altar railings were set up and curtains hung, one attached to the altar canopy, the other at the pergola of the choir screen, which in smaller churches were simple wooden beams (see Fig. I). The reason for all this grew out of the belief that the mystery occurring on the altar had to be shielded from the eyes of men.

The Byzantine picture wall (*iconostasis*) is really nothing more than an evolution of the choir screens (*cancelli*) of the early Christian Church. The *iconostasis* is generally equipped with three doors, as are the *cancelli* constructed during the reign of the Emperor Justinian (who died in 565) at the Hagia Sophia Church in Constantinople. These choir screens, just as those made in following centuries, show pictures of Christ and Mary, angels, prophets, and apostles. From the same period is the famous Christ icon at the Sinai Monastery, which, if we consider its size (84 centimeters) probably came from such an early *iconostasis*. Icons were and still are installed between the pergola columns, or sometimes, as for example the so-called *Deiisis* (Christ shown between Mary and John the Baptist), they are placed on top of these columns. The use of curtains (*vela*), which had always been a part of the altar, and the choir screen, were finally discontinued during the Baroque period when the architectural design of churches emphasized light and sweeping views. To cite some evidence from actual documents, at the end of a rubric for the consecration of a church found in the Sacramentary of Angoulême (c. 800), we read, "After this, the altars are draped (with cloth) and the curtains of the temple (*vela templi*) are hung" (see Duchesne, *Origines*, 3rd Edition, p. 485). Similarly, we find a reference in the rite for consecrating a church in the Drogo *Sacramentarium* describing a velum being hung between the church nave and the altar (*inter aedem et altare*) (Duchesne, *Origines*, p. 488).

It is important that we again learn to show respect before the altar.

In the Eastern as well as the Western Church, it is customary that the priest when approaching the altar makes a deep bow; in the Book of Exodus (29:37), it says about the altar in the holy of holies, "Whoever touches the altar must be treated as holy." Jesus, too, says that it is "the altar that sanctifies it (the offering)," and that we should only place our offering on the altar after having made peace with our brothers (see Mt. 5:23).

During the offering of the Sacrament of the New Testament, the altar becomes the throne of God. Thus, St. John Chrysostom reminds his listeners, "Think about who it is that enters here. Start trembling even before you see Him. Because everyone who beholds the (empty) throne of God, his heart is moved as he awaits the King's entrance" (PG 61:313).

In the early Church (and during later periods, too), a circular lamp hung in front of the altar canopy, and a golden (or silver) receptacle mostly fashioned into the shape of a dove in which the Eucharist was kept, mostly for use in distributing Communion to the sick. Also in early use for reserving the Eucharist was a small box, fashioned after the Ark of the Covenant of the Old Testament (*arca*), of acacia wood overlaid with sheets of gold (Ex. 37:1-9). A beautiful example of such a box is kept in Chur; it was made in the late eighth century. Dating from the ninth century is the golden ciborium of Emperor Arnulf, originally kept at the St. Emmeram Church in Regensburg, now in Munich. It features four small columns, very similar in design to the *artophorion* (tabernacle) found on the altars of Byzantine churches to this day.

These receptacles were always on the altar or in a niche located in its back. The altar tabernacles of our time, made of metal, evolved from these original forms. As late as the thirteenth century Durandus mentions, in his *Rationale divinorum officiorum*, the positioning of an *arca* on the altar, "where the Body of the Lord and holy relics were stored (together)" (*De altari*, I, 2, n. 2). The practice of storing the Host in a small house designed specifically for the Eucharist located on the left wall of the choir area is a much later development, which was observed primarily during the Gothic period. To keep the Holy Eucharist right on the altar makes eminent sense, although to store it in another eminent place in the church building would not present a problem.

As Nyrus of Ancyra (died in 430) observed (PG 79:577ff.), at the top of the apse wall, above the throne for the bishop and the seats for the priests, there was only the cross; and this arrangement continued unchanged at least until the fifth century; or, as we can still see in some Roman mosaics, in addition to the cross, there was an illustration of Christ as teacher, surrounded by His Apostles. Later, in the West— and this was quite common until the Gothic period—we see Christ enthroned in the mandorla of the rainbow, surrounded by the four living creatures mentioned in the Apocalypse (4:8 ff.) and by angels; under that, in a row, we see the Mother of God, the Apostles and other saints representing the community of heaven.

During the celebration of the Eucharist, the faithful saw the picture of Christ enthroned in heaven, and so they knew that He was with them. Apparently, it was not enough to simply remember the word of the Lord, "For where two or three meet together in my name, I am there among them" (Mt. 18:20)—it had to be expressed visually, as a picture.

Fig. 2. The sanctuary of the Cathedral of Parenzo (Istria), sixth century, showing the upper half. (Drawing by Jupp Palm.)

An apse wall devoid of all pictures, as we have it now in many modern churches, was unthinkable then. After the new church had been built, the first wall to be painted was the apse wall, before any other wall in the building was decorated with paintings or mosaics. To name but a few examples, we must mention the splendid mosaics found in the basilicas of Ravenna, and in the cathedrals of Venice, Torcello and Parenzo. (See Fig. 2.)

We have observed that the paintings in the apse served first and foremost as cult images: they were a symbol of the risen Lord present among His people. The paintings on the walls of the nave depicted scenes from the Old and New

129

Testament, as seen from a Western perspective, and served as a means to instruct the people about salvation history.

In contrast, in the Byzantine East illustrations of this type are primarily designed to make the mysteries of salvation relate to the here and now. This is indicated by the many pictures of saints displayed on columns and on other walls: they represent the presence of the heavenly community or reflect that we are to be admitted into that community (see Hebr. 12:22).

In the Orthodox Church, the church interior is the place where past, present and future come together, where eternity appears in the *Hodie*, the Today—a word used at the beginning of many hymns—the place where heaven and earth are united. (See Fig. 3.)

As already explained, in the Western Church the faithful who were assembled to celebrate the Eucharist saw the picture of the transfigured Son of God and the cross as the symbol of our salvation. The cross was first and foremost a symbol of victory, as the "sign that heralds the Son of Man" (Mt. 24:30), at the end of time, and as such had to be decorated with gold and precious stones. Its place was either on the altar, or behind it; and until the Romanesque period, it did not have the Corpus attached to it.

It was not until later that it became customary to paint the image of Christ crucified upon the cross, or to attach it to an enamelled representation; and even then it was not the sorrowful Christ dying from his terrible sufferings, but Christ who had vanquished death or Christ as the High Priest. The realistic images of the anguished body, which eventually became the norm in the Western Church, were rejected as a matter of principle in the East because, it was believed, they overemphasized Our Lord's human nature.

Since, based upon this traditional view, the representation of the glorified Son of God in the apse, and the cross placed either on or above the altar, were always understood as

Fig. 3. The Monastery Church Nerezi near Skopje (formerly Yugo-slavia).

fundamental elements in the decoration of the sanctuary, there has never been the least doubt that the gaze of the celebrant, while offering the Holy Sacrifice, must have been directed towards the East, towards the cross and the image of the transfigured Christ, and not towards the faithful participating in the celebration, as is now the case when Mass is celebrated *versus populum*, facing the people. Few modern churches have such a focal point. In fact, it appears that contemporary artists have an aversion to the depiction of realistic images in churches. This is a result of the inner conflicts that are tearing modern man apart, and that render him incapable of creating sacred art. In the end, what is really lacking in our Western Church is the tradition that in the Eastern Church continues to form the basis for the liturgical cult as well as for the building of churches and the creation of liturgical art.

In the Orthodox Church, the task of the artist is first and foremost to produce the essential, the traditional picture— that of the mystery of salvation—as it has been described in Holy Scripture and passed down to us by tradition. This prescribed task discourages the artist from "doing his own thing"—a tendency rampant in modern church art—but does not stifle his creative spirit.

Unlike the Eastern Church, the design of the sanctuary and the altars in the Western Church has, over time, gone through a number of changes. For example, during the late Romanesque period, and especially during the Gothic period, altars began to be modified by setting a background panel on the altar, a practice that ultimately developed into the very high background panels (*reredos*) we see attached to the typical Baroque altar.

In the aftermath of the Second Vatican Council, this particular feature of the altar has been subject to a profound change, indeed, as we cannot fail to notice in many of our churches.

Following the Council, many churches removed the communion rail, which represented what originally had been the choir screen, to make room for an "altar of the people," which was added to the already existing high altar, for the celebration of Mass facing the people. And wherever you turned, there were microphones! A microphone on the altar, at the *sedilia*, at the lectionary stand. The pulpit was no longer used.

This new style in the design of the sanctuary has been replicated in a surprisingly uniform way on almost all continents. While in older church buildings the "altar of the people," the *sedilia* and the lectionary stand were designed as moveable objects to be set up in the sanctuary, in new and reconstructed church buildings they have become permanent fixtures representing what is considered to be a "modern" church design.

The Holy Eucharist is reserved in a tabernacle installed on a wall behind the altar or on its left. The new altar facing the people is made of stone and positioned in such a way that it allows only a celebration of Mass facing the people. Such an altar, the *sedilia* for the priest, also frequently fashioned of stone, and the massive lectionary stand—all tending to be of questionable artistic merit—certainly do not reflect tradition!

There would, of course, have been many models from past centuries that could have provided inspirations for new church designs, and particularly for new altar designs.

E. A. Lengling has described the "Tendenzen des deutschen katholischen Kirchenbaus aufgrund der Beschlüsse des 2. Vatikanischen Konzils" ("Emerging Trends in the Design of German Catholic Church Buildings in Accordance with the Decisions of the Second Vatican Council"), in his essay of the same title appearing in *Liturgisches Jahrbuch* (*Liturgical Yearbook*), published in 1967. The demands for change that were made in this book have by now been commonly accepted and implemented. No serious attempt had been made to justify these changes historically, with the possible exception of the study done by Otto Nussbaum, which we will discuss later.

Finally, a comment about the practice of celebrating the Eucharist at large outside gatherings under the open sky. There are many among the faithful who feel very uncomfortable at such assemblies, primarily because of the manner and form in which Communion is administered on such a large scale.

In considering this practice, we must remember that while Christ preached to large crowds of people, probably numbering in the thousands (Mt. 14:21), he chose to institute the Holy Eucharist not in the presence of multitudes of people but in the small circle of his Apostles.

It was the consensus of all Christians, never challenged, that the Mass, the Holy Sacrifice that brings together heaven and earth, had been instituted to be celebrated only in especially designated, sacred rooms. We also know that the Jewish Passover Lamb was to be eaten only inside of a building, not out in the open (Ex. 12:46).

Aside from these theological and liturgical considerations, there is also a practical one: the obvious difficulties of having ready and consecrating the number of hosts needed to distribute Communion to many thousands, even hundreds of thousands of people. The simple and rather obvious solution to this dilemma would be not to offer Communion to the people assembled in such large numbers, but this option has been rejected out of hand because of the erroneous assumption that if we understand the purpose of the Mass to be that of a communal meal, the distribution of Communion to the faithful is an indispensable part of all Masses.

What does not make sense at all is to see liturgical worship conducted out in the open when large churches are readily available for the same purpose. Practices such as these deliberately reject a Church tradition that is more than 2,000 years old. They also contradict the true purpose and function of the

Holy Mass, which has always been understood as a sacrifice and as a mystery. To celebrate this "Mystery of Faith," we should go inside the protecting walls of our churches where the *Mysterium* is kept safe. The sacred character of such a designated place can then create in us a proper attitude toward that which is holy—a sense that can only exist in a person who approaches it with great reverence.

XIV

The Altar Facing the People: Questions and Answers

There was another angel that came and took his stand at the
altar, with a censer of gold; and incense was given him in
plenty, so that he could make an offering on the golden altar
before the throne, out of the prayers said by all the saints.
(Apoc. 8:3)

According to the Letter to the Hebrews, the Temple of Jerusalem was God's temple on earth, and the temple with its
altar was a representation of the Heavenly Sanctuary, the
Sanctuary into which Christ has come as the eternal High
Priest (Heb. 9:24).

The liturgy of heaven and earth are joined into one. The
quotation from the Apocalypse tells us that an angel is standing before the golden altar in heaven, holding in his hand a
golden censer to offer incense together with the prayers of
the faithful on earth before God Himself. Seen in this context,
we can even say that the sacrifice we are offering to God here
on earth will be acceptable to Him only if it is "carried by
your holy angel to your altar on high," as we pray in the
Roman Canon.

The concept that the altar here on earth represents the real altar before God's throne in heaven, has always determined its position in our churches and the position of the priest standing before it: the angel with the golden censer is standing *before* the altar. Clearly, this notion is also based on the instructions that God gave to Moses (see Ex. 30:1-8).

These introductory observations are necessary to illustrate to what extent modern thinking about the altar has changed and differs from the traditional view. The change did not happen suddenly; it developed gradually and its origins go back to the years preceding the Second Vatican Council.

Theodor Klauser, in his *Guidelines for the Design of the House of God According to the Spirit of the Roman Liturgy* (1949), says:

> There are some indications that in the church of the future, the priest will again be standing behind the altar and will celebrate Mass facing the people, as is still being done in the old Roman basilicas. It is this clear desire to more strongly emphasize the concept of the communal meal which makes this approach necessary.

What Klauser described as a desirable change has now become common practice. And many are under the impression that this change simply represents the revival of an early Christian practice. But we can show with certainty that there has never been, neither in the Eastern nor the Western Church, a celebration *versus populum* (facing the people); rather, the direction of prayer has always been towards the East, *conversi ad Dominum* (turned toward the Lord).

The idea that the priest is to face the people during Mass has its origins with Martin Luther, in his little book, *The German Mass and Order of Worship* (1526). At the beginning of the chapter entitled, "The Sabbaths for the People," he writes:

Let all the vestments, the altar, the candles be, until they get used up, or we decide to change them. And if some-body wants to do things differently, let him do it. But for the real Mass among true Christians, the altar should not remain in its current form and the priest should always face the people—as, we can undoubtedly assume, Christ did during the Last Supper. Well, all this will come to pass in time.

That time has now, indeed, come to pass....

In writing about the celebrant's position at the altar and how it should change, Martin Luther, the reformer, refers to Christ's own behavior during the Last Supper. Apparently, Luther envisioned the scene of the Last Supper in the frame-work of his own time: Jesus standing or sitting at the center of a long table, the Apostles placed at His right and left.

Can we positively say that this is how Jesus actually sat at the table?

What we can say is that He probably did *not*—simply because it would have contradicted the table etiquette ob-served in antiquity. At the time of Jesus, and during the following centuries, no round or semi-circular tables were in use. The side of the table facing the observer remained empty: it was the side from which the food was served. The people partaking in the meal would sit or recline behind the table, in a semi-circular arrangement, resting on sofas or on a semi-circular bench. The place of honor was not, as one would expect, at the center of the table, but on its right side. The second highest place of honor was at the opposite end of the table. This seating arrangement is depicted in all the oldest illustrations of the Last Supper, up to and into the Middle Ages: the Lord is always reclining or sitting at the right hand of the table (see Fig. 4).

It was in the thirteenth century that a new type of illustra-tion appears: Jesus is now sitting behind the table, in a center

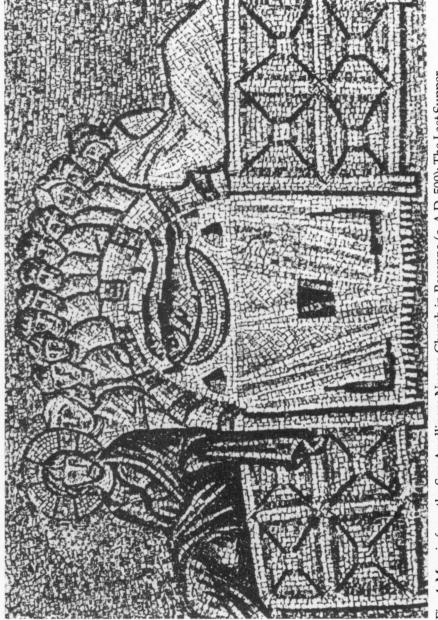

Fig. 4. Mosaic from the San Apollinare Nuovo Church in Ravenna (c. A.D. 500): The Last Supper.

position, surrounded by His Apostles. It is this picture that Luther had in mind.

It is true that this type of illustration looks very much like a celebration *versus populum*, yet the impression it gives is wrong because, as we all know, "the people" whom the Lord would have been facing were not in the room in which the Last Supper took place. Luther's argument is simply invalid. Incidentally, as far as we know, Luther himself never insisted on the celebration facing the people: that practice developed later and then only in the parishes of the Protestant Reformed Churches.

First Question

This may all be true. But what about the situation in the early Church? Didn't the faithful all sit together with their Leader at "The Lord's Table"?

To answer this question, we have to draw a distinction between the celebration of the Agape, the Communal Meal of Love, and the celebration of the Eucharist, which in the earliest times of Christianity *followed* the Agape meal, but later *preceded* it. I discuss this point in detail in my book, *Beracha*.

During the first centuries, when the number of the faithful in a community was still small, the seating order used during the Agape meal carefully followed the order used during the Last Supper—which is not surprising, considering that at the time, this was part of common table etiquette anyway. This seating arrangement can also be discerned from the foundations of a number of early Christian house churches excavated in some rural Alpine regions: there is the relatively small room located in the center of the building, approximately 5 meters by 12.5 meters in size, and at its center is a stone bench of semi-circular shape, designed to accommodate 15 to 20 persons. These findings have been presented in a detailed and comprehensive study that appeared under the title, *The Patriarchy of Aquileia and the Bavarian Church*.

In the towns where larger numbers of faithful needed to be accommodated during worship, several tables would be set up. The bishop and the presbyters would sit at one table, while the faithful, separated by sex, would sit at the other tables. There is a reference in the Letter to the Galatians (2:11-21) where the Apostle Paul reproves his brother apostle Peter for having, in Antioch, sat down together at the table with the Christians of Jewish origin, purportedly avoiding the tables of the Christians of pagan origin.

While during the communal meal—the Agape—people sat at the table, during the celebration of the Eucharist the people got up and stood behind the celebrant at the altar, as specifically prescribed in the *Didascalia Apostolorum*, a Church procedures manual of the second and third century, a manual which also instructs the faithful to turn toward the East (II 57, 2-58, 6, in the Funk edition).

During the following stages of development, the communal meal is discontinued (since about the fourth century) and the tables disappear. At that point, the faithful were sitting on benches placed along the walls of the church chamber and the wooden altar table now becomes an altar made of stone.

Second Question

How can anybody be against the altar facing the people, since its use has been prescribed by the Council and it has been established everywhere?

One would look in vain for a statement in the *Constitution on the Sacred Liturgy* of the Second Vatican Council that said that Holy Mass is to be celebrated facing the people. Back in 1947, Pope Pius XII, in his encyclical *Mediator Dei*, pointed out that the person "who wants to change the altar into the old form of the *Mensa* (the table) is going down the wrong road." The celebration of the Mass *versus populum* was not allowed until the Second Vatican Council, but many bishops quietly tolerated the practice, particularly during Masses celebrated specifically for young people.

In Germany, the new place of the priest *behind* the altar had its beginnings in the *Jugendbewegung*, the youth movement of the 1920s, when it was popular to celebrate the Eucharist in small groups. A pioneer of this practice was Romano Guardini at the Masses he celebrated at Burg Rothenfels. The liturgical reform movement, with Pius Parsch in the vanguard, also did its part to promote the popularity of this practice. In Klosterneuburg, near Vienna, Parsch set up a small Romanesque church (St. Gertrud) for this very purpose, for his very own "liturgical community."

Practices like these were finally sanctioned by the *Instructions on the Proper Implementation of the Constitution on the Sacred Liturgy* in the document *Inter Oecumenici*, issued by the Congregation of the Holy Rites in 1964; and these instructions also found their way into the new Missal. For church buildings to be newly constructed, the following was prescribed:

> Normally, a church should have a fixed and dedicated altar, freestanding, away from any wall, so that the priest can walk all around it and can celebrate facing the people (cf., *General Instructions on the Roman Missal*).

Unfortunately, it is true that the new altar facing the people has been established worldwide, that is, in those areas where the Roman Catholic Church is established. But it is also true that these altars are not actually prescribed.

The orthodox Eastern Churches, which, after all, have a membership of hundreds of millions of believers, continue the early Christian practice, which has the priest and the faithful facing the apse during the celebration of the Holy Sacrifice. This is also true for Churches following the Byzantine rite (the Greeks, Russians, Bulgarians, Serbs, etc.), as well as for the old Oriental Churches (the Armenians, Syrians, Copts).

The issue of whether the altar should be freestanding so that "the priest can walk all around it" is a different matter entirely. This particular part of the "Instructions" of the Liturgy Commission certainly agrees with Church tradition.

For more than ten centuries, the altar in the West—as it remains to this day in the orthodox Eastern Churches—did not have a *reredos*, a superstructure. This change came later, during the Gothic period when the triptych altars with side panels began to appear. This type of altar displayed the paintings that had been on the apse and the other church walls, and illustrations depicting events from salvation history spanning the whole cycle from the Annunciation to the Ascension of our Lord.

We have already observed that up to and into the Gothic period, the altars in smaller churches were often attached to the apse wall, while in the larger churches they were situated at the center of the sanctuary. In this way, the priest was able to actually walk around the altar, when, for example, censing the altar, just as it says in Psalm 25:6, "I will...go about your altar, Lord, praise of you in my ears and all your wonders on my lips."

To enhance the holiness of the altar, particularly in the larger churches, we find a beautifully worked canopy resting on four columns. At the four sides of this canopy, curtains were hung; and this was most certainly modeled after the curtain in the Temple at Jerusalem, which separated the Holy of Holies (*Sancta sanctorum*) from the Sanctuary, *per se*, in accordance with God's instructions to Moses in Ex. 26:31-33.

In the Byzantine rite, this separation is represented by the *iconostasis* decorated with icons, which, according to the Orthodox, also represents the *Ecclesia caelestis,* the union of the faithful with the Heavenly Church, and thus is not only seen as a separating wall, but also as a focal point for those partaking in the celebration.

The *iconostasis* does not exist in other, non-Byzantine rites of the Eastern Churches. Taking its place, for example among the Armenians, are two curtains: a small one before the altar and a large one that shields the entire choir area from the view of the faithful. These curtains are used during certain parts of the liturgy of the Mass. According to St. John Chrysostom, "When you see the curtains being drawn, think of the heavens above opening up and the angels descending."

Based on the reports of Durandus in his *Rationale divinorum officiorum,* such curtains were also used in the West until the Middle Ages. He mentions three "veils": one covering the offerings, the second around the altar, and the third in front of the choir.

While in the early Church the altar was intentionally shielded from view, albeit with precious cloths and *antependia,*[121] in today's church the altar is situated in the middle of the room, undecorated, exposed to the view of everybody. Does this really present the altar as the holy place where the sacrifice is being offered? Certainly not! Rather, contrary to all tradition, what is being stressed now is the altar as a meal table.

---

121 *Antependium*: a vesture (or frontal) that hangs in front of the altar, usually varying in color to correspond to the changing ecclesiastical seasons.—Trans.

In that case, the real purpose of the Mass is not to bring what is eternal into our temporal world; rather, it is about man and his world of the here and now. The world of God and His angels and saints is only of peripheral interest and carries little meaning. At best, there is an interest in the Person of Jesus as a human being, and in selected excerpts from His Gospel!

Third Question

But isn't it true that during the Middle Ages, there was, in addition to the High Altar, also an altar for the people?

This is true in the sense that beginning with the late Romanesque [*Spätromanik*] period, we commonly find in cathedrals and monastery churches an "Altar of the People" placed in front of the rood (choir) screen. This screen was a kind of cloister wall for the choir, but somewhat higher than those found in early church buildings, with an entrance on each side of the altar for the canons or the monks, who were thus separated from the rest of the church. Because of the cross that was commonly a part of the screen and set above this altar (more precisely, was set on top of the screen in the rood loft), the altar was commonly known as the "Cross Altar."

In these churches Mass was celebrated for the people on this altar, as were all the Masses at which large congregations were present, such as solemn funeral Masses or, in cathedrals, the coronation of the sovereign (see Fig. 5). Homilies were delivered from the top of the rood screen (rood loft). The high altar inside the sanctuary behind the rood (choir) screen was reserved for the solemn Masses of the community.

The purpose of the rood (choir) screen was not so much to function as a barrier between the clerics and the people

Fig. 5. The coronation of the wife of the Emperor Ferdinand II before the "Lettner" (Lectionary) at Regensburg Cathedral, showing the use of the "cross altar" (copper etching of 1630).

but to create a room for the canons or the monks where they could conduct the liturgical duties of the choir, e.g. the praying of the Divine Office as well as the Masses for the community. For this reason, we cannot really compare the function of the Byzantine *iconostasis* with that of the rood screen.

The removal of the rood screen together with the "Cross Altar," which in Germany was done almost universally at the command of the secular authorities during the "Enlightenment," was not a good idea, liturgically or architecturally; see my paper on this subject which appeared in *The Cathedral* (1985).

147

The major architectural changes made to church interiors during that time period—the intent must have been to provide the faithful with a good view of the High Altar—reappeared in our time, following the conclusion of the Second Vatican Council, when almost none of the older church buildings were spared "renovation."

A person traveling around visiting different churches is bound to encounter some rather unusual approaches to the redesign of the sanctuary. One example, applying to many Italian Baroque churches, was to leave the *reredos* itself intact but to remove the entire altar table, putting in its place the *sedilia* [seats] for the celebrant and his assistants. This solution turned out to be one of the least appropriate because the *reredos* had now lost its relevance to the Eucharistic Sacrifice for which it had been created, its significance having been lessened by simply serving as a backdrop for the *sedilia*.

In most situations, however, what used to be the High Altar now only serves one purpose, or more precisely, its tabernacle serves that purpose: as the place where the Holy Communion hosts are being reserved. Nobody seems to see anything wrong with the priest standing at the *mensa* altar facing the people and having his back turned to the tabernacle, which, until recently, was a focal point for the praying faithful. Sometimes the church choir will be standing on the steps leading up to the High Altar. They, too, have their backs turned to the tabernacle, and they may even use what was once the altar table as a convenient place to park their music scores and other assorted items.

Except for cases where historical considerations made this impossible, the entire High Altar has been removed and the Eucharist is being kept in a tabernacle installed on a side wall. But that arrangement raised the question of what to do with all the empty space that had been created in the apse. A number of different approaches were developed. In many cases, the organ, together with its decorative encasement, was installed here, as were the members of the church choir. Alternatively, the original *reredos* or the artistic *antependium* were used as decorations and hung on the apse wall.

In the end, all these solutions turned out to be unsatisfactory, simply because the placement of a new altar, which was often purposely simple in design, destroyed the sense of balance in spatial relationships intended by the original architect, a balance that relied on the High Altar as its center and its focal point. A. Lorenzer is right when he observes in his book, *The Council of Accountants*, "For the interior space of a church, the position of the altar is of such great significance...that its repositioning would require a complete redesign of the room's spatial relationships."

This is particularly evident in such large churches as the Kaiserdom at Speyer where, upon entering, the visitor's eyes were first drawn to the (former) High Altar and its canopy. Today, the visitor sees an empty space. In spite of its relatively large size, the new *mensa* altar situated in the choir area is hardly conspicuous in the high space of the church's interior. The altar facing the people which is located on a platform a couple of steps down, does not present itself as a "spatial focal point or center."

Fourth Question

In his Guide to Liturgy for the Pulpit, School and Home *(1926), P. Alfons Neugart says that, "In the basilica of the early Church, the altar was situated at the center of the choir apse, and the priest-celebrant had his place behind it, facing the people. There was neither a cross, nor candlesticks on the altar. Along the walls, there were seats for the bishop and the clerics. It was only later that the altar was placed against the wall as we know it today."*

It is true that during the first centuries the seats for the bishops and priests were located not along the sides of the sanctuary but along the apse wall. In Greek church buildings the seats were elevated by several steps so that the bishop when sitting on his throne could be seen by all present, and also so that the people were better able to hear him when he delivered his homily from his throne. The center seat in this arrangement was always reserved for the bishop, a practice still observed in the Eastern Church.

It is also true that originally there was no cross, no candlestick and no missal on a stand on the altar. The only items on the altar were the chalice and paten containing the sacrificial offerings. We know this from many different medieval illustrations that show the celebration of Mass. Until our days, flowers had been used to decorate the church floor, but never the altar.

The altars were quite small, having a top surface of less than one square meter. For example, there is a small, solid stone altar from a very early period located in the crosswalk outside the Regensburg Cathedral. Inside, in the original part of the cathedral, there is a comparatively large altar from about the fifth century with a surface dimension of 2.1 meters by 1.4 meters. This identifies it as a *Confessio* altar, that is, it was built above the grave of a martyr, which explains its large size.

The small surface of most of the old altars was to provide room only for the sacrificial offerings of bread and wine. This characteristic underlined the unique character of the Mass as a sacrificial act, just as among the Jews and pagans only the offerings were placed on the altar.

In the early Church, large *mensa* altars were uncommon. But even the *mensa* altars, like the so-called block altars, were always covered with richly decorated covers extending over all sides and reaching down to the floor so that the altar's table shape was not readily discernible. During later times a decorated *antependium* made of wood or metal or other material was attached to the front side of the altar. In light of these facts, no convincing argument can be made that the early *mensa* altars were an indication of the communal meal character of Mass.

We will address the issue of the position of the priest at the altar in the early Church at a later point and in greater detail. But we want to quote from Fr. Josef A. Jungmann, the author of the well-known book, *Missarum Sollemnia*, published shortly after the conclusion of the Second Vatican Council, in the magazine, *The Pastor*. The author writes, "The claim that the altar of the early Church was always designed to celebrate facing the people, a claim made often and repeatedly, turns out to be nothing but a fairy tale."

Jungmann also warns us not to allow the mere *approval* to use the so-called altar facing the people to be made into "an absolute requirement, and in the end to become the standard, readily accepted by all without due deliberation." He identifies the primary reason why facing the people has become the one and only, the preferred way to celebrate Mass: "Above all else, this represents an emphasis that has become so very popular and at the same time so very one-sided and exclusive: to see the Eucharist as a communal meal." In the same way, Josef Cardinal Ratzinger has, over the past few years, pointed to the growing danger of seeing the liturgy "only under one single aspect: that of the 'brotherly meal.'"

Fifth Question

Hasn't the pope himself, since time immemorial, celebrated Mass facing the people; and doesn't St. Peter's Basilica in Rome have an "altar island," just as most of our contemporary churches do?

While the design of the Baroque St. Peter's Basilica would certainly appear to suggest the idea of an altar island, that was not the case in the design of the original St. Peter's Basilica built by the Emperor Constantine. In its present form, the elevated pontifical altar stands in an open space, right in the center under the cupola that rises over the *confessio*, the grave-site of the Prince of the Apostles. The altar can be seen from all directions, that is, from the main nave, as well as from the side naves.

All those who have attended pontifical Masses have noticed for some time that, unlike in the rest of Christendom, the pope did not stand before the altar but behind it. This observation was used as the basis on which some liturgists speculated and arrived at the erroneous conclusion that this must be a vestige of an early Christian practice—that of celebrating Mass facing the people.

As we will explain shortly, the real explanation for this is the ancient custom of facing East in prayer, with St. Peter's Basilica, unlike the great majority of churches, having its apse facing West, rather than East.

Studying photographs that show the pontifical altar before it was remodeled by Pope Paul VI, we immediately notice the huge candelabra and altar cross, which made it almost impossible for the faithful to see the pope standing behind the altar. Considering this, we cannot seriously maintain that what we had here was a celebration *versus populum*. Neither are we dealing with a special privilege exercised by the pope, as is sometimes asserted: in Rome there are a number of other churches with the apse facing West, and in these churches, the priest is also standing behind the altar.

In modern churches, that is, in churches built after the Second Vatican Council, we often encounter an altar island, similar to that of St. Peter's, the main difference being that in the modern churches there is no canopy, which would have been the altar's crowning glory. As a real "island," floating in the middle of nowhere, and surrounded on all sides by the bench seats of the faithful, it is difficult to find a suitable place for the altar cross. We have already described the basic purpose of the altar cross as a focal point; and also that the new liturgical directions require it. This is what it says in the *Institutio generalis* of the new Missal: "Above the altar or in close approximation to it, a cross should be affixed that is clearly visible to all the faithful." (See n. 270).

This condition was certainly met at the medieval "cross altar." It is not met by seeking to comply with the instruction in a makeshift fashion, e.g., by placing a small cross on the *mensa* altar, either in an upright position or, as is sometimes done, by laying it flat on the altar surface.

Sixth Question

Was it really the right thing to do, having the priest direct his prayers to a wall? Isn't it a much better idea to have him face the people?

When standing before the altar, the priest does not pray to the wall: he prays to the Lord together with all the assembled faithful.

Until recently, Christians were less concerned about forming a "faith community" than in the priest offering the Sacrifice before God as the representative of the faithful and together with them.

Saint Augustine says this about the direction of prayer:

When we raise our hearts in prayer, we turn towards the East (*ad orientem convertimur*), whence heaven arises. This is not to say that God could (only) be found there and that he has forsaken the other directions of the world..., rather, we face East to remind ourselves that we must turn in the direction of a higher natural state, that is, that we must turn to God.

This statement tells us that in those days the faithful would stand for prayer after the homily had been completed, and turn to face East. In fact, when concluding his sermons, St. Augustine would frequently call on his assembled listeners to turn to the East, using a set formula, *conversi ad Dominum* (turn to face the Lord). All this is reminiscent of what St. Paul had to say on the subject. Knowing that "so long as we are at home in the body we are exiles from the Lord," he wants to be "exiled from the body and make our home with the Lord (*ad Dominum*)" (2 Cor. 5:6-8).

In the early Church, to turn and face the Lord and to look towards the East was one and the same thing.

In his indispensable book, *Sol Salutis*, published in 1920, Joseph Dölger expresses his conviction that the response by the faithful, *Habemus ad Dominum* (We have lifted them up to the Lord), which follows the priest's call, *Sursum corda* (Lift up your hearts!), also implies turning and facing the East, that is, "facing the Lord."

Dölger points out that in some Oriental liturgies there is a special call that the deacon makes immediately prior to the Eucharistic Prayer (*anaphora*) inviting the faithful to turn towards the East. This applies, for example, to the Coptic *Basilius-Anaphora*, which says at its beginning, "Come close, you men, stand in reverence and look towards the East!"; or to the Egyptian *Marcus-Anaphora*, containing a similar call, "Look towards the East!" which is part of the Eucharistic Prayer, recited prior to the *Sanctus*.

The practice of rising to pray and facing the East during prayer is specifically mentioned in a short description of the liturgy that is part of Book 2 of the *Apostolic Constitution*, published in the fourth century. In Chapter 8, the appropriate call made by the deacon is rendered as, "Arise and face the Lord!"

Here, too, we see the parallel association between the act of turning to face East and facing the Lord. Dölger has also pointed out that the custom of praying in the direction of the sunrise is an ancient one, practiced by Jews and pagans alike.

The Roman author Vitruvius wrote this in his treatise about architecture (I, 4,5):

> The direction that the temples of the immortal gods should be facing should be such that...the image (of the god) to be set up in the temple's *cella* (the Holy of Holies) should look out towards the setting sun so that those who stand in front of the altar to offer a sacrifice or to perform (some other) sacred act, are facing the eastern sky and at the same time are also facing the god's image inside the temple.

To face East in prayer was a common practice for Tertullian, circa A.D. 200, as well. In his tract *Apologeticum*, he speaks of Christians "praying in the direction of the rising sun." The proper direction in which to turn for prayer was indicated early on by a cross placed on a wall in people's houses. Such a cross has been found in the upstairs room of a house buried by the eruption of Mount Vesuvius in A.D. 79, in the city of Herculaneum.

Seventh Question

But has there not been research—that of Professor Otto Nussbaum, for example—scientifically proving that the practice of celebrating Mass facing the people was used in the early days of Christianity; in fact, that this practice was the original way of celebrating Mass?

In his voluminous study, *The Position of the Priest at the Christian Altar* (1965), Nussbaum says, "Ever since buildings have been constructed that were specifically designed for liturgical worship, there has been no firm rule about on which side of the altar the priest should stand. At times he could stand in front of the altar, at other times, he could stand behind it." Nussbaum then offers his opinion that until the sixth century, the celebration of Mass facing the people had been the generally preferred practice.

Unfortunately, Nussbaum fails to make a clear enough distinction between church buildings with the apse facing East and those with the apse facing West—in the latter case, with the entrance facing East. Churches with the apse facing West and the entrance facing East are almost exclusively the basilicas of the fourth century, and among them predominantly those which were built by the Emperor Constantine and his mother St. Helena —for example, St. Peter's in Rome.

As early as the beginning of the fifth century, however, St. Paulinus, Bishop of Nola, reports that having the apse facing East was the "usual" way of building churches. Consequently, we find churches with their entrances facing East primarily in Rome and in North Africa, while they are relatively uncommon in the East, i.e., in Tyre and Antioch.

The practice of having entrances face East in the churches built under the Emperor Constantine follows the design of the Temple of Jerusalem (Ezek. 8:16), as well as the design of some temples of antiquity, which allowed the light of the rising sun to shine into the temple chamber and illuminate the image of the god inside.

In Christian basilicas with the entrance facing East, the celebrant had to stand at the "back" of the altar, in order to offer the Holy Sacrifice towards the East, while in churches in which the apse faced East, the priest always stood "before" the altar (*ante altare*), his back to the people.

The fact that in many of the basilicas we have mentioned the altar provided enough room for the priest to stand behind has often been used to support the argument that this was, in fact, where he had been standing, facing the people, especially if the *sedilia* for the priests and a bishop's throne were placed along the apse wall. This argument is not correct, and unfortunately Nussbaum employs it too. There are several case studies, all firmly grounded in archaeological research findings, that prove it wrong. Indeed, if this argument were true, why would any churches have been built which have a precise orientation towards the East?

Eighth Question

But if in churches with the apse facing West (St. Peter's in Rome) the priest did stand "behind" the altar, was this not in fact a celebration facing the people?

The answer is: No! For the simple reason that during the Eucharistic Prayer, the *Canon Missae*, it was not only the priest who was facing East, but also the people. St. John Chrysostom observed long ago that since antiquity the faithful joined the priest in lifting up their hands in prayer (see Fig. 4) and everyone was turned to gaze at the open doors through which the light of the rising sun was streaming into the church's interior—the rising sun being the symbol of the risen Lord returning.

Aside from the special awe that the Emperor Constantine, the builder of this church, reportedly had for the sun, there is also a statement made by the prophet Ezekiel that certainly played a role: "The man led me to the gate that faced East, and there, *coming from the East*, was the glory of the God of Israel" (Ezek. 43:1).

Just as the Lord appeared to his disciples on several occasions after His Resurrection when they were assembled for the communal meal (Lk. 24:36-49; Jn. 21; Acts 1:4)—so the people who had come together for the celebration of the liturgy were awaiting the return of Christ through the doors of the basilica, which opened towards the East.

The faithful—men separated from women—traditionally did not stand in the center nave but in the side naves—there were up to six of those in some large basilicas; the Lateran Church and St. Peter's in Rome only have four side naves.

Fig. 6. Mosaic from Thabarca in North Africa, Fourth Century: Ecclesia mater (according to DACL IV, 2). The altar is situated in the middle of the center nave.

The custom of the faithful standing in the side naves traces its origin to the seats that were lined up against the side walls of the small house churches during the early days of Christianity, a practice that, incidentally, is still in use in the Eastern Churches. The center nave or the space under the central cupola was reserved for liturgical functions. The older people among the faithful would be sitting on the seats (*stasidia*) that were lined up against the side walls of the side naves; the other people would attend the worship service standing. Unlike the position of kneeling, which until recently, had been the appropriate manner of worshiping in our churches, in the East it is standing during services which is considered proper, a posture which, it must be noted, demands considerable physical discipline, particularly during services lasting a long time.

We can see from archaeological excavations and from relevant illustrations (see Fig. 6) that in the basilicas built under the Emperor Constantine and in North Africa the altar was situated approximately at the center of the center nave.

The altar was enclosed by choir screens and usually surmounted by a canopy. The choir (*scola cantorum*) stood facing the celebrant. In the churches of Ravenna, although they are all, without exception, oriented toward the East, the positioning of the altar and of the choir in the center nave continued for some time, demonstrably until the eighth century (see Gamber, *Liturgie und Kirchenbau* [*Liturgy and the Building of Churches*], pp. 132ff.).

Even the altar of St. Peter's in Rome, built by the Emperor Constantine, was not situated as one would expect over the grave site of the apostle, but approximately in the middle of the center nave. At the location where the Prince of Apostles was buried there was a *Memoria* crowned by a canopy resting on columns, but no altar. We can see this depicted in an early illustration on the small ivory casket of Pola (see Fig.7). There is no proof to support the frequently made assertion that a portable high altar was standing at the location where the pilgrims were coming and going to visit the apostle's grave site.

In the basilicas with the apse facing West rather than East, and with the altar situated in the middle of the center nave, the faithful who were standing in the side naves did not have their backs turned towards the altar: because of the holiness of the altar this would have been something unthinkable. With little physical effort, the faithful were able to turn their bodies in the direction of the East, towards the church entrance.

Even in the unlikely event that the assembled faithful did not, during the Eucharistic Prayer, face the entrance but the altar, that still would not have resulted in the priest and the people facing one another since, as we have already observed, in the early days of Christianity, the altar was shielded from view by curtains.

Beginning in the Middle Ages, the altars in the basilicas we have mentioned were moved closer to the apse. We know

Fig. 7. The apse of the old St. Peter's Basilica in Rome, prior to its reconstruction under Pope St. Gregory the Great (Reconstruction based on the ivory tablets of Pola.)

Fig. 8. Reconstruction of the Altar of St. Peter's Basilica in Rome under Pope St. Gregory the Great, circa 600 A. D., according to Rohault de Fleury, Confessions. In front of the altar, surmounted by the canopy is a type of screen decorated with pictures

that in St. Peter's this occurred under Pope St. Gregory the Great, who around A.D. 600 also ordered a major reconstruction of the choir area and caused the ring crypt to be built so that the pilgrims could more easily visit the grave site of the apostle, without having to enter the sanctuary (see Fig.8).

Over time, the faithful would gradually move into the center nave. Ultimately, the faithful in the basilicas that had been built under Constantine began to face not East but rather the altar—we cannot tell for certain when exactly that began to happen—and this over time gave the *impression* that Mass was celebrated facing the people.

Ninth Question

In churches with the apse facing East (which, as we know, was true for the vast majority of early church buildings), what was the position of the priest and of the faithful?

In the basilicas that had an apse facing East and also had several side naves, the faithful would, at least originally, stand in the side naves and also in the rear part of the center nave. In this way, they formed a semi-circle open towards the East, with the celebrant standing at the center of the (imaginary) full circle.

By comparison, in the basilicas that had an apse facing West, the priest, surrounded by attending clerics and members of the choir, was situated at the vertex of this imaginary semi-circle. Later, when the faithful increasingly moved into the center nave, they resembled an army formation, and a certain dynamism was created, something like the procession of the people of God through the desert towards the Promised Land. Facing East was to indicate the direction in which the procession was to move: towards paradise, which had been lost and which was to be found again in the East (see Gen. 2:8). The celebrant and his assistants were at the head of this procession.

In contrast, the earlier formation of the faithful in an open semi-circle expressed a stationary principle: the waiting for the Lord who, having ascended to the East (see Ps. 67:34; Zech. 14:4) will come again from the East (see Mt. 24:27; Acts 1:11). When we expect the arrival of an important person, the group of waiting people will form into a semi-circle to receive the expected person into their midst.

In his *De fide orthodoxa* (IV, 12), John of Damascus says:

When ascending into heaven, He rose towards the East, and that is how the Apostles adored Him, and He will return just as they saw Him ascend into heaven, as the Lord has said: 'Just as the flash of lightning rises from above and then descends downward, so will be the arrival of the Lord.' Waiting for Him, we adore Him facing East. This is an unrecorded tradition passed down to us from the Apostles. (PG 94:1136).

Since about the sixth century, we find this view expressed in the subject chosen for the paintings in the main cupola of the apse in many churches: the Ascension of the Lord. A particularly good example of this are the paintings of that time period at Bawit in Egypt. At the upper part of the painting we see Christ in His Glory, carried by two angels; below, there is Mary representing the praying Church, her hands raised up towards heaven, and to her left and right, we see the Apostles. This illustration was meant to represent both Christ's glorification in heaven and His *parousia*, His Second Coming, as announced by the two angels to the Apostles at His Ascension to Heaven, "This Jesus who has been taken from you up to heaven will come in the same way as you have seen Him go" (see Acts 1:11; see also Gamber, *Sancta Sanctorum*, pp. 31ff.).

In the apse paintings of the West, the image of the enthroned Christ appearing in a mandorla was later cast into the new setting of *Majestas Domini*. Here Christ sits surrounded by the four living creatures mentioned in the Apocalypse (4:8 ff.) which became the normative form of apse painting in Romanic church art. In the Byzantine churches of the East, Christ was portrayed as the Lord ascended to heaven, either in the form of the Pantokrator painted in the main cupola, or in a setting showing the entire Ascension scene on the curved wall above the altar. However, it is interesting to note that in almost all paintings that did extend to the curved wall below the cupola, the Mother of God remained a part of the main apse painting (see Fig.2).

This central position which Mary occupied in the apse paintings may well have been based on the text taken from the Apocalypse, "God's sanctuary in heaven was opened, and within His sanctuary was seen the ark of His covenant" (as described earlier, this ark stood on the altar as a vessel containing the Eucharist). "After that there appeared a great sign in heaven: a woman robed with the sun, beneath her feet the moon, and on her head a crown of twelve stars" (Apoc. 11:19, 12:1).

Worth noting in this connection is the relationship between the figure of Maria-Ecclesia and the ark of the covenant; and further, that the temple curtain, that is, its Holy of Holies, was only to be seen on special occasions. It seems that what is being ignored and forgotten all too easily today is that a mystery—the *tremendum*—in order to be a mystery, needs to be hidden, so that we may long for it to be revealed.

The Apostle Paul writes, "At present we see only puzzling reflections in a mirror, but one day we shall see face to face" (1 Cor. 13:12). Our orientation towards the East is not only a looking out for the Lord glorified in heaven and returning to us at the end of time; it is also our longing for the revelation of all things at the end of time, and the final realization of the glory yet to come.

Tenth Question

Contrary to the contention that we always faced East during prayer, and that this was the reason why churches were built facing East as well, there is the fact that in the oldest Roman basilicas the altar and the apse can be found facing in all possible directions. How can this be explained?

Some churches were either built on existing foundations that remained from antiquity, or built based upon some local peculiarity that did not allow the church to be precisely set along an East-West axis. But that did not stop the priest and faithful from following the old Christian practice of jointly turning and facing towards the East during prayer and the Sacrifice.

For example, the well-known church of San Clemente in Rome is built on a foundation from antiquity and its entrance faces south-east. For that reason, the celebrant in this church had his place at the back of the altar. A celebration with the priest standing in front of the altar would have been impossible because of the church's particular layout. But, standing behind the altar to face East during the Holy Sacrifice, the priest only had to turn his body very slightly to face that direction. This also applied to the faithful standing in the side naves; in the center nave of San Clemente is the designated area for the *schola* (choir), and also the two *ambones* (raised platforms), one for reading the Epistle and the gradual, the other for reading the Gospel.

Louis Bouyer observes that "The idea that the Roman basilica is the ideal design for a Christian church building because it made it possible for the priest and the people to face one another is complete nonsense. That would have been the last thing that the early Christians had in mind."

At any rate, the line of reasoning on which this question is based ignores the practice of building churches facing East during the fourth and fifth centuries, a practice that cannot be explained unless this orientation was related to the direction of praying.

To support the view that the altar with the cross standing on it is the focal point towards which the faithful are drawn and around which they should be assembled, the text *et omnium circumstantium* (and all here present gathered round), which is part of the *Memento vivorum* (Remember the living) prayer in the Canon, is often cited as proof.

Addressing the philological part of this argument, we can say that the expression *circumstantes* can be taken to mean

Fig. 9. Mosaic from the Church of San Marco, Venice. Prayer petitions being offered for the recovery of the lost relic of St. Mark (twelth-thirteenth century).

quite generally "all here present," or "all standing about," and not necessarily "all who are standing around forming a circle." There is no mention in the literature that could lead one to believe that during the celebration of the Mass the faithful were actually standing in a circle around the altar; nor would that have been possible, because lay people were not allowed to enter the sanctuary, a prohibition that still applies in the Eastern Churches.

Reverence can only develop in an environment where appropriate behavior is considered to be important, even if such behavior has to be brought about through prohibitions and limitations designed to keep in check the profane. If, for example, a sacristan thinks nothing of putting a chair or ladder onto the *mensa* of the altar in order to place a candlestick or flowers in the upper niches of the *reredos*, the sanctity of the altar would certainly be grossly violated. To do this would be completely unthinkable in the Eastern Churches!

By contrast, the expression *et omnium circumstantium* can remind us of the proper behavior which the faithful should show when the Sacrifice is being offered—that is, to stand in reverence (see Fig. 9). In our time, the "standing about" has turned into "sitting" on permanently installed seats in modern churches, a tempting convenience. Of course, to bring about a change in this established practice would be difficult; nevertheless, we should always remember that to stand was the original liturgical position, a position that, incidentally, also tends to encourage a greater sense of community, particularly if people stand together in a group, away from the rows of seats and benches bolted to the floor.

Eleventh Question

All this is certainly laudable, but can modern man really be expected to have an appreciation for the practice of facing East during prayer? No longer does the rising sun have the symbolic signifi-

cance it had for the man of antiquity; or even for a person living in a Mediterranean climate who probably experiences the life-giving effect of the sun much more intensely than the northern European. For today's Christian, the concept of the "eucharistic community around the table" has much greater significance.

Even if modern man is no longer concerned about the exact direction in which he faces during prayer—although even today, Muslims are still facing Mecca and Jews continue to pray towards Jerusalem—he should, nevertheless, understand the reason why the priest and the faithful should both be facing in the same direction.

The idea that all who participate in offering the Holy Sacrifice should join together "facing the Lord" is a timeless one; and it makes good sense even in our day and age. Aside from the theological issue involved in having the priest facing the people during the celebration of the Eucharistic sacrifice, there are also some sociological problems we need to consider relating to the issue of creating the "eucharistic community around the table."

Professor of Sociology W. Siebel, in his short work, *Liturgie als Angebot* (*Liturgy On Offer*), expresses his belief that the priest facing the people "represents the best and primary symbol of the new spirit in liturgy."

He continues,

....the practice (of the priest facing the other way) that had been in use before gave the impression that the priest was the leader and representative of the faithful acting as a spokesperson for the faithful, like Moses on Mount Sinai. The faithful assumed the role of sending a message (prayer, adoration, sacrifice); the priest functioned as the leader delivering the message; God as the recipient of the message.

In his new role, continues Siebel, the priest

> is hardly continuing to function as the representative of
> the faithful, but as an actor who plays God's role, at least
> during the central part of the Mass, similar to what is
> played out in (the) *Oberammergau* (Passion Plays) and in
> other religious plays.

Siebel draws this conclusion:

> This new turn of events having changed the priest into
> an actor expected to play the role of Christ on stage, in
> the re-enactment of the Last Supper, makes the persons
> of Christ and the priest merge in a way that heretofore
> had been impermissible.

Siebel explains the readiness with which almost all priests
accepted the *versus populum* celebration:

> The considerable level of insecurity and loneliness expe-
> rienced by the priest naturally brings about a search for
> new emotional support structures. A part of this emo-
> tional support is the support provided by the faithful.
> Yet, this support also leads to a new form of dependency:
> the dependency of the actor on his audience.

In his article, "Pubertätserscheinungen in der Katholischen Kirche" ("Signs of Puberty in the Catholic Church"), K.
G. Rey observes something quite similar:

> While in the past, the priest functioned as the anonymous
> go-between, the first among the faithful, facing God and
> not the people, representative of all and together with
> them offering the Sacrifice, while reciting prayers that
> have been prescribed for him—today he is a distinct

person, with personal characteristics, his personal life-style, his face turned towards the people. For many priests this change is a temptation they cannot handle, the prostitution of their person. Some priests are quite adept—some less so—at taking personal advantage of a situation. Their gestures, their facial expressions, their movements, their overall behavior, all serve to subjectively attract attention to their person. Some draw attention to themselves by making repetitive observations, issuing instructions, and lately, by delivering personalized addresses of welcome and farewell...To them, the level of success in their performance is a measure of their personal power and thus the indicator of their feeling of personal security and self-assurance. (p. 25).

Siebel, in *Liturgy on Offer*, picks up on the view advanced by Klauser, cited above, that the celebration *versus populum*, "serves to more clearly express the eucharistic community around the table," saying,

The intended coming closer together of the people around the Lord's Supper table hardly contributes to a strengthening of the sense of community. It is only the priest who is actually at the table, and standing at the table, at that. The other participants in the supper are sitting, closer or farther removed, in the auditorium.

To this, Siebel adds another observation:

Usually, the altar table is situated at a distance and it is elevated, which means that the sense of togetherness that existed in the room where the Last Supper took place simply cannot be re-created. Facing the people, it is difficult for the priest not to give the impression that he is trying very hard to sell us something. To correct this impression, attempts are made to move the altar into the midst of the faithful. In that way, the individual does not have to look just at the priest, he can now also look at the person next to him or at the person sitting across from him. Moving the altar into the midst of the faithful, however, also means that the space between a sacral center and the faithful is being lost. The holy fear that used to seize us when entering the church where God was really present, is replaced by weak sentiment, a response to something that is little more than ordinary.

From a sociological point of view, placing the priest behind the altar, facing the people, turns him into an actor, totally dependent on his audience, and also into a salesman offering his wares to the public.

Alfred Lorenzer, in his book, *Das Konzil der Buchhalter* (*The Council of Accountants*) brings out some other issues that, to some extent, deal with aesthetic matters:

And it is not only that the microphone picks up every breath that is being drawn, together with every other background noise. The whole scene is more reminiscent of the studio setup for a television cooking show; even the liturgical forms observed in Protestant Reformed Churches are more formal. In the Reformed Churches, the ritual became marginal, it was purposely brought to a level of simplicity and brevity. The liturgical reform (in our Church) has kept the sacred rite at the center of its liturgy, while doing away with the treasure of the symbolic acts that are an integral part of it. It goes on to present awkwardly the rite as an essential process of deliberate acts; it insists on conjuring up a false sense of transcendence that confuses the physical act of doing something with the real transcendental nature of the mythos. For example, it is intent on purposely exhibiting an act which shows us every detail of the ritual of eating: you sit and watch a man awkwardly breaking the brittle Host into pieces, and you watch how he stuffs the pieces into his mouth. Whether you like it or not, you are forced to witness the way the person chews—not always an aesthetically pleasing act to watch; you get to watch the person's peculiar way of [consuming the Sacred Species],...you watch his way of drying and polishing the chalice with a cloth" (p. 192).

That, in short, is the social aspect of the priest facing the people while celebrating Mass. Of course, the reading of the Word of God is a different story. Here the priest's position of facing the faithful is a given, just as it has always been understood and accepted that the priest delivering his homily faces the people, as does the deacon when singing the Gospel.

We have already noted that the actual Liturgy of the Eucharist is altogether different. Unlike the Liturgy of the Word, which is, if you will, a presentation to the people, the Liturgy of the Sacrifice is a holy act wherein heaven and earth unite and God's grace flows down to us. Here, the direction of the participant and that of the priest-celebrant must be focused in prayer on the Lord. It is only during the Communion of the Faithful, which is the Eucharistic meal in its true sense, that we again have the priest come face to face with the communicant.

This alternating change in the position of the priest at the altar during the celebration of the Mass has an important symbolic and social significance. During prayer and sacrifice, the priest, together with the people, should face God; but when he proclaims the Word of God and gives Communion, he faces the people.

As we have seen, the custom of facing East in prayer is as old as the Church; it is a tradition that cannot be changed. It symbolizes a continuous "looking out in the direction of the Lord" (J. Kunstmann), or, as Origen says in his tract about praying (c. 32), it is "an allegory of the soul looking towards the beginning of the true light, 'looking forward to the happy fulfillment of our hope when the splendor of our great God and Saviour Christ Jesus will appear'" (Tit. 2:13).

Twelfth Question

Why is the nature of the Mass as a sacrifice less evident when the priest is facing the people?

A counter-question: Since experts concede that today's use of the altar facing the people cannot be legitimized by any reference to ancient custom (i.e., that such an altar had actually been used by the early Christians), why can we not accept the inevitable conclusion drawn from this insight and remove all the "meal table" altars that have been set up with surprising uniformity all around the world?

The answer to this latter question is very obvious: it is the newly created understanding of the *nature* of the Mass and the Eucharist, which differs markedly from the traditional one.

The deliberate purpose is to avoid giving the impression that the "Holy Table," as the altar is called in the Eastern Churches, is, in fact, a sacrificial altar, an altar on which to offer the Holy Sacrifice. This is the most likely reason why the contemporary altar is usually prepared in a manner reminiscent of a table set for a formal family dinner: there is the (single) vase with flowers and two or three candles. The candles are mostly grouped at the table's "left side," while the bouquet of flowers are placed at the opposite end.

This asymmetrical arrangement is deliberate: what is to be avoided here is the creation of a focal point that in the past was created by the altar cross at the center of the altar and the candlesticks placed on its right and left side. After all, the current aim is to make the altar into a meal table.

You stand *before* an altar on which a sacrifice is to be offered. You do not stand *behind* it. This simple concept was even apparent to the priest offering a sacrifice in pagan times. The priest faced the image of the god in the temple's inner sanctuary, the god to whom the sacrifice was being offered. This basic approach was quite similar to what occurred in the Temple of Jerusalem. The priest whose task it was to offer the animal sacrifice stood before the "Table of the Lord" (Mal. 1:12), as the great altar in the center of the temple yard was called, facing the inner temple where the Ark of the Covenant was kept in the Holy of Holies, the place which was the abode of the Most High (see Ps. 16:17).

A meal takes place with the head of the family sitting among the members of his family, or to use a different term, within the family circle. A sacrifice, however, is offered using a liturgy specifically created for that purpose; and it is offered inside or in front of a sacred place (which could be a sacred tree). Again, this basic concept applies to all religions. The liturgy is raised above the people; its proper place is in front of the people, in front of the altar, before God's countenance.

Throughout history, people have turned in the direction of the one for whom the sacrifice was intended. They did not turn in the direction of their fellow men. How the early Church thought about this matter is described by Origen, in his explanations of the Book of Numbers (10:2): "The person standing before the altar indicates through his position that he is engaged in priestly functions. It is the priest's office to pray for the forgiveness of the people's sins." Unfortunately, this is a perception that is of little consequence in today's world, where our awareness of sin and of our sinful state seems to have been largely lost.

It is commonly known that Luther rejected the nature of the Mass as a sacrifice. He thought Mass to serve the primary purpose of preaching the Word of God, with the *Abendmahl*, the commemorative meal, to follow—which serves to explain why he called for the already cited turning of the liturgist to face the congregation.

While it is true that Catholic theologians generally do not *directly* deny the nature of the Mass as the offering of a sacrifice, a number of them do insist that the sacrifice should not be its central purpose; and that instead, the concept of the communal meal be emphasized during the celebration of the Mass. This they do primarily for ecumenical reasons, so as not to offend the Protestants; apparently, they don't mind offending the sensibilities of the Eastern Orthodox Churches, which believe that the nature of the Divine Liturgy can never be anything else but the offering of the Sacrifice.

A real change in the contemporary perception of the purpose of the Mass and the Eucharist will occur only when the table altars are removed and Mass is again celebrated at the high altar; when the purpose of the Mass is again seen as an act of adoration and glorification of God and of offering thanks for His blessings, for our salvation and for the promise of the heavenly life to come, and as the mystical reenactment of the Lord's sacrifice on the cross.

We have already pointed out that this does not mean that the Liturgy of the Word cannot or should not be conducted away from the altar, at the *sedilia* or the lectionary, just as has been done during pontifical Masses. But all prayers should be said facing East, that is, in the direction of the image of Christ in the apse and of the cross on the altar.

Since, during our pilgrimage here on earth, we are unable to understand the true magnificence of the mystery being celebrated, let alone to see Christ Himself and the "community of heaven," it is not enough to simply *talk* about the solemn character of the Sacrifice of the Mass; rather, we must do everything we can to demonstrate the magnificence of the event to the people—through the celebration itself, and through the artistic decoration of the church, above all of its altar.

We can apply what Dionysius the Areopagite has said in his book, *About the Holy Names* (1, 4), about the "holy veils" and how they apply to both the event of the cult itself and to the images. The "holy veils," he says,

> conceal from us that which is spiritual and what from the next world is present in this world. They give image and form to that which has neither form nor image...but later, when we have become perpetual and immortal and have found our rest in Christ, we shall forever be, as Scripture says, with the Lord (1 Thess. 4:17), totally consumed by beholding His real image.

Our discussion should have established that the practice of the priest facing the people during the celebration of the Holy Sacrifice cannot be documented anywhere, from any source—until Martin Luther, that is—and that there is no archaeological evidence to support it, either.

The actual expression *versus populum* (facing the people) first appears in an official text in the "The Rite to be Used When Celebrating the Mass," which is part of the *Missale Romanum* revised by order of the Council of Trent under Pope St. Pius V, published in 1570. Section V, 3 of this text addresses the situation of "the altar facing East [not towards the apse of the church but] towards the people" (*altare sit ad orientem, versus populum*), a situation which, as we have already mentioned, applies to a number of old churches in Rome.

The emphasis of this passage is on the term *ad orientem*, a fact that is today conveniently ignored. In the text, the phrase *versus populum* is but an attribute relating to the immediately following instruction, which says that in this particular case the celebrant, when offering his *Dominus vobiscum*, need not turn around (*non vertit humeros ad altare*), because he is already facing the people he is addressing. The priest's position of standing "behind the altar," which occurred in some Roman basilicas, led, as we have already mentioned, the priests of the German Catholic youth movement of the 1920s to the erroneous conclusion that this was a practice observed by the early Christians, a practice that had somehow survived in Rome.

Just as in the Western Church, celebration *versus populum* has never existed in the Eastern Church—there is not even a term that could be used to describe it. It is worth mentioning in this connection that during concelebration (which, as we know, has a long tradition in the Orthodox Church), the main celebrant stands, as always, with his back to the people, while the co-celebrating priests position themselves to his left and right. In no case, however, do they stand at the altar's back side, that is, at its East side.

However, we must not hide the fact that even in the Eastern Churches there have been movements, some of them continuing, that would have the liturgy celebrated facing the people or at least to place the altar in front of the iconostasis. The perils associated with such changes and their effect on the proper conduct of worship were clearly recognized by the Patriarch Tichon of Moscow in 1921. Responding to the reforms advocated and practiced by some priests after the Russian Revolution, he wrote in a pastoral letter addressed to all bishops in his country:

> All this is done under the pretext that the liturgy has to be adjusted to meet the demands of our time, to revitalize our worship, and thus to attract the faithful and bring them back into our churches. We withhold our blessing for violations of this kind, from the self-styled activities of a few individuals conducting their own form of litur-

gical worship services. We do not give our blessing, *because we cannot do this in good conscience.* The divine beauty of our liturgy, as it has been set down by the Church in her ritual manuals, her rubrics and her instructions, must remain intact and inviolate in the Russian Orthodox Church, *because they are our greatest and most holy possession.*

Time has proven the Patriarch right. The fact that the Russian Orthodox Church still exists, that she is, indeed, flourishing, is due primarily to her faithfully maintaining and cultivating her traditional liturgy.

The deciding issue concerning the position of the priest at the altar is, as we have said, the nature of the Mass as a sacrificial offering. The person who is doing the offering is facing the one who is receiving the offering; thus, he stands *before* the altar, positioned *ad Dominum*, facing the Lord.

If, nowadays, the aim is to emphasize the aspect of the communal meal during the "Eucharistic Feast" by celebrating *versus populum*, this aim is not being met, at least not in the way some might have hoped. The new arrangement has the "meal leader" positioned at the table, by himself. The other "meal participants" are situated in the nave, or in the "auditorium," not directly connected to the "meal table."

In small groups, it has become increasingly popular to have all participants stand around the altar in a circle, a practice that serves to completely destroy the meaning of the Mass as a sacrificial offering. The best way to correct this is to do what has been done since time immemorial: to join the priest as he "faces the Lord," that is, to face in the same direction.

Our Faith holds that holy Mass is more than just a communal meal celebrated in memory of Jesus of Nazareth. The central factor is not that a community is brought together and that we experience a sense of community—although the importance of such an experience should not be underestimated (1 Cor. 10:17)—but the liturgical worship of God.

The focus must forever be on God, not man. This has always meant that everyone turn towards Him in prayer, rather than that the priest face the people. From this insight, we must draw the necessary conclusion and admit that the celebration *versus populum* is, in fact, an error. In the final analysis, celebration *versus populum* is a turning towards man, and away from God.

Fig. 10. The Mass of St. Erhard, Evangelary of the Abbess Uta
(partial view), eleventh century.

XV

The Mass of Saint Erhard:
An 11th-Century Miniature from Regensburg

With His body, He nourishes in faith the Church here on earth,
He who also nourishes the angels in heaven with His Countenance.
(Inscription on the Miniature)

The miniature painting shown in Fig.10, which is taken from a Regensburg manuscript of the eleventh century now located in Munich, depicts the (central) sanctuary of a church design common in Western Europe during the Middle Ages. We see St. Erhard, one of the bishops of Regensburg before St. Boniface's time, celebrating the Mass. The miniature is part of the manuscript and appears on Folio 4r; facing it on the opposite (left) side, on page 3v, is the illustration of a symbolic Crucifixion showing Christ hanging on the cross dressed in an alb and wearing a stole. The presentation of the painting of the Crucifixion on one page and that of the Mass on the opposite page is intentional (see Beissel, *Geschichte der Evangelienbücher (The History of Evangelaries)*, p. 258ff).

In the illustration, Bishop Erhard is standing before a *mensa*-style altar, covered with precious cloths, under a canopy resting on four columns. On the *mensa*, aside from the chalice and the paten, we see only an *evangelarium* and a ciborium for the Eucharist. Hanging from the canopy is a circular lamp that served as a decoration for the altar as well as a source of light. In the background, we can see a curtain, decorated with crosses.

We are certain that the miniature painting was a part of the *ornatus palatii*, the palace treasure of Emperor Arnulf, which he presented to the monastery of St. Emmeram in Regensburg towards the end of the ninth century. What remains of these treasures is the priceless *evangelarium*, the famous *codex aureus*, and the altar-ciborium, both now located in Munich

The miniature illustration includes a faithful reproduction of the actual ciborium, and from it we can see that the small box that is hanging from its top and was used to store the Eucharist is now missing; see Gamber, *Ecclesia Reginensis*, pp. 176ff.

In those days, an *evangelarium* was part of the altar's essential liturgical appointments—as it continues to be in the Eastern Churches to this day. It was this book from which the deacon would sing the Gospel, and since it contained the Lord's own words, the intent was to make it as valuable an object as possible—with magnificent bindings and miniature illustrations in the text. There are, in fact, manuscripts extant with silver and gold letters written on purple parchment.

From a ciborium that still exists, we can tell that it was not intended to be moved, but rather was a vessel designed for housing the Eucharist; we can tell this by reading the text that appears in the miniature painting directly above it, written on the inner part of the altar's canopy:

Sancta sanctorum (Holy of Holies)

Iesus Christus, verus panis, veniens de caelis (Jesus Christ, true bread, which comes from heaven)

Hic pascit ecclesiam corpore suo per fidem in terris, qui per speciem suam angelos pascit in caelis (With His Body, He nourishes in faith the Church here on earth, He who also nourishes the angels in heaven with His Countenance).

At this point, we should also cite the instruction given by Pope Leo IV (847-855), which said, "Nothing must be placed on the altar other than the container with the relics, the *evangelarium* and the pyx containing the Body of our Lord" (PL 115:667).

St. Erhard is portrayed in his full episcopal regalia. In addition to an amice, or cowl, which is not visible, he is dressed in an alb, the priest's stole, and a maniple at his left hand; on top of these clothes he is also wearing a deacon's dalmatic with a deacon's stole, its end pieces visible on the left side. He is also wearing a bell-shaped chasuble, and on top of that, the *rationale*, a type of pallium that has been worn by the bishops of Regensburg since time immemorial and continues to be worn by them to this day (see Gamber, *Ecclesia Reginensis*, pp. 184ff.). On his head, Bishop Erhard is wearing (an early form of) a miter with the two lappets attached to it hanging down to his shoulders.

The assisting deacon is wearing the vestments common for his rank, including the maniple. The stole is under his dalmatic. To have a deacon assist the priest during Mass was then a common arrangement. St. Isidor of Seville writes that,

the Levites take the offerings to the altar; they prepare the table of the Lord; they lock the Ark of the Covenant (which means, the Eucharistic pyx). They also give the chalice to the faithful (*De eccl. off.* II, 8; PL 83:789).

A short comment about how Masses were commonly depicted in illustrations at that time: As we can see in the illustration, the artists, particularly those in the East, liked to show the celebrant from a frontal aspect. By doing this, they risked giving the impression of the priest standing in a position of facing the people; this observation also applies to the famous ivory tablets in Frankfurt. As we can see from Illustration IX, and also from the illustration of the book's frontispiece in the West, a side aspect was preferred in representations of this type during early times; it was uncommon to show a priest celebrating Mass having his back turned to the people.

Addendum

The Concept of the Sacrifice of the Mass in the Early Church
Or, Why the Translation of "For You and For All" Is Wrong

For this is my blood, the blood of the (new) covenant, shed for many for the forgiveness of sins. (Mt. 26:28)

When we bless the cup of blessings, is it not a means of sharing in the blood of Christ? (1 Cor. 10:16)

Is the translation of the Latin, *pro vobis* and *pro multis*, in the words of consecration, which appear in almost all vernacular editions of the new Missal as "for you and for all," the correct translation? The issue is still being debated. Some insist that, primarily for philological reasons, the translation must necessarily be "for all," while others see that translation as an obvious falsification, indeed as a dangerous attack on the faith. They maintain that "for all" is a heresy originating with Origen, who held that in the end everyone will be saved (*apokatastasis panton*). In fact, this argument contends that to use falsely the very words spoken by our Lord, words that are to bring about the transubstantiation of the sacrificial offering into His Body and Blood, is to put into the Lord's mouth what is clearly a heresy, thus rendering the Mass invalid.

To examine this issue, we must first define two distinct elements. The first is God's clear intent to redeem mankind, which St. Paul denotes in 2 Cor. 5:15, when he says, "He died for all...." In his exegesis of the Gospel, Eusebius of Caesarea says (I, 10), "(The blood of Christ) is the great and full ransom that pays for the sins of the Jews, as well as for those of the pagans; it is the atonement for the whole world, the token of life for all mankind." (PG 22:87).

The second element concerns the question whether all mankind will, in fact, be saved; that is, the essential difference that exists between God's intended redemption and the acceptance of Christ's redeeming grace by the individual person. St. John Chrysostom has this to say in his exegesis of the Letter to the Hebrews:

Although (Christ) died to, as far as He is concerned, save all, His death voiding the downfall of all mankind, yet He did not take away the sins of all, because they themselves did not want Him to do this (PG 63:129).

To these two primary elements—that is, that Jesus died for all mankind, and whether all mankind will actually be saved—we must add a third: the actual meaning of the text used for the consecration in the Missal, i. e., the concluding part of the Mt. 26:28 passage, "for this is my blood, the blood of the covenant, shed for many for the forgiveness of sins" (*qui pro vobis et pro multis effundetur in remissionem peccatorum*). It is this third element that will be the sole basis for the following discussion. We will analyze the problem strictly as a question of liturgical science.

Before we get into this discussion, however, a comment on the merit of the philological argument used to justify the translation "for all." The argument is made that the cited text passage in Mt. 26:28 actually is a Semitic idiom, according to which the text can be taken to mean "many" or "all." What is missing here is the article to "many," which is essential if we are to assign the correct meaning to the term. And even if there were an article, the Greek expression οι πολλοι could only in some instances be translated as "most of them," but most certainly not as "all"—so says Blass-Debrunner in his *Grammatik des neutestamentlichen Griechisch (Grammar of Greek for the New Testament)* (245). To support his view, Blass-Debrunner cites Mt. 24:12, "the love of many (= of most) will grow cold."

It is equally important to note that there is not a single old translation of the Mt. 26:28 passage, and not a single liturgical consecration text used in the many different oriental liturgies, that uses the translation "for all." Another significant factor: "for all" does not even appear in the German standard translation. The only reference we can find is in the rather liberal translation of the New Testament called *Die gute Nachricht (The Good News)*, published in 1967, which says on page 75, "This is my blood, which is shed for all men for the forgiveness of sins." This may well be the source of "for you and for all," which found its way into the new German Missal.

We can conclude that on a philological basis, no valid argument can be made to justify the translation "for all." This means that we will need to examine the meaning of the words actually spoken by Jesus. Doing this, we must take note of the fact—and this is important—that in contrast to the Matthew text (and also to the Mk. 14:24 text, "This is my blood, the blood of the covenant, shed for many"), the text of Lk. 22:20, says, "This is the cup, the new testament in my blood, which shall be shed for you." So that in the passages by Matthew and Mark, we have the "for many," and in the Luke text, the "for you." In 1 Cor. 11:25, St. Paul altogether leaves out the second part of the words of consecration containing the contested passage.

Based on the versions of the words of consecration in the Gospels of Matthew and Luke, the following text gradually came into the Roman rite, and it developed this way in similar rites as well: "This is the cup of my blood, of the new and everlasting covenant, the mystery of faith, which shall be shed for you and for many for the forgiveness of sins."

The question that concerns us at this point is this: why does Matthew say "for many," and Luke say, "for you?" What did Jesus actually say when He offered the cup to His disciples?

The commonsense assumption we can make about this is that the Lord was addressing only the Apostles when He said, "for you." This interpretation would also correspond to the passage in Lk. 22:19 (or in 1 Cor. 11:23), "This is my body, which is for you;" and lead to the conclusion that in both instances, in the chamber where the Last Supper was held, Jesus gave His body (as a sacrifice) and shed His blood "for the forgiveness of sins." It would then follow that the words spoken by Jesus, "shed for you," were directly addressed to the Apostles, just as "for many" applied to those communicants who, during the following years, would approach the eucharistic chalice "for the forgiveness of sins" and so receive the grace of salvation.

Since, however, the Lord shed His blood not only for the Apostles or the communicants, but as it says in the institution of the original consecration rite on Maundy Thursday, "for the salvation of all mankind" (*pro omnium salute*), it follows that the passages, "which is for you," relating to the consecration of the bread, and "shed for you," relating to the consecration of the blood, are not directly linked to the Lord's death on the cross.

Christ's Blood in the chalice, which the Apostles drank, was indeed the Blood (albeit in transfigured form) which would be "shed" on the cross the next day; it was given to them at that time as a sacrament, "shed for the forgiveness of sins." In the same way, His Body which would be given up in sacrifice on Golgotha (and be transfigured by His Resurrection), was "given up," and given to them in the form of eucharistic bread as food; it was, as most translations of the 1 Cor. 11:24 text passage describe it, actually "broken."

In this context, we have to remember that the death of Jesus on the cross is the Sacrifice made by the God-Man, and that it was made once, "in the fullness of time" (Eph. 1:10), but that it was also and at the same time an eternal act of the Son giving Himself to God the Father, to God for whom "there is no variation, no play of passing shadows" (Jas. 1:17), for whom time does not exist, because everything is present. Accordingly, Christ is the Lamb "predestined before the foundations of the world" (1 Pet. 1:20) to be slaughtered for us. It is for this reason that Jesus was able to invite the Apostles to drink of His Blood as a sacrament while referring to His Sacrifice on the cross, although that event, in terms of earthly time, was not to occur until the next day. As the Syrian *Afrahat* (*Festschrift* Maria Höfner, p. 12) said, in the chamber where the Last Supper was held, "Our Lord has given us with His own hands, His Body as food and His Blood to drink (even) before He was crucified."

That the words used for the consecration of the wine have been interpreted as simply serving the utility of our salvation, and not primarily being sacramental in nature, is because they have not been linked to the words of consecration used for the bread, that is to say, that it was "given up for you," or "broken."

The early liturgical texts display a much clearer understanding of all this. For example, the famous papyri of Der Balaisa, in which large parts of a Eucharistic prayer, probably dating back to the third or fourth century, have been preserved, both words of consecration, when compared to the

189

traditional biblical texts, are perfectly symmetrical in form, "Take it and eat it, all of you: this is my body, given up for you for the forgiveness of sins, " and, "Take it and drink from it, all of you: this is my blood, shed for you, for the forgiveness of sins" (Hänggi-Pahl, p. 126). The study published by Fr. Hamm in 1928, *Die liturgischen Einsetzungsberichte (The Words of Consecration and Institution)*, maintains that this is also true in most of the anaphorae of the Eastern Church, but that enhancements of the original texts did occur later.

We can assume that the phrase "for many," used by Matthew and Mark and the later Eucharistic Prayers of the Eastern and Western Church, in lieu of or as the presumably original text passage "for you" appearing in the Luke Gospel, and also appearing in the Der Balaisa papyri, is based on the recitation of the Lord's words of consecration used during the eucharistic breaking of the bread in the primitive Church. What we have here is a liturgical adaptation, an example of different linguistic and idiomatic formulations of the words of consecration and institution contained in the New Testament, formulations that indicate their early use as part of liturgical worship among the faithful.

By using the phrase "for many" instead of "for you," the purpose was to address the "many" faithful that were now participating in the liturgy, just as Jesus directly addressed "all" the apostles then assembled in the chamber where the Last Supper was held, to drink from the eucharistic chalice.

In 1 Cor. 10:17, St. Paul, too, makes use of the word, "many," when he speaks about receiving the liturgical bread i.e., that, "we, though many" (i.e., those receiving the liturgical bread), "are one body," in Christ. In this passage as well, the theme is the grace given to those receiving the Body of Christ; it is only indirectly about the redemption on the cross.

One reason, and an important one at that, why the current predominant view that the words "forgiveness of sins" refer directly to the redemption on the cross—a view that made it necessary to also change the text to "for all"—rather than the act of grace flowing to those receiving the precious Blood, can be found in the fact that the Greek word εκχυννομενον ("is being shed"), has been translated in most Latin Vulgata editions—but not in most of the Vetus-Latina Codices—in the future tense, i.e. as, *effundetur* ("will be shed") instead of *effunditur* ("is being shed"). Using the future tense does, of course, emphasize the Sacrifice on the cross and at the same time de-emphasize the act of grace flowing out of the drink-ing of the eucharistic Blood, "for the forgiveness of sins." The *effundetur* ("will be shed") version that appears in the original Greek translation, subsequently found its way into the *Mis-sale Romanum*—which, of course, first created this problem.

J. Pascher, in his *Liturgisches Jahrbuch No. 10 (Liturgical Yearbook No. 10)*, published in 1960, also points (p. 99 ff.) to the fact that the Greek word εκχυννομενον, "to shed," does not carry the meaning of "the flowing of blood out of a wound," but rather means "to pour out," as we have already translated that term. During the celebration of the Eucharist, the Lord's precious blood is "poured out" of the chalice into the mouths of the (many) faithful, in the same sense as the Old Testament blood sacrifice was consummated only by the act of "the pouring out of the cups."

In this context, we must also cite a passage from the sermons of *De sacramentis*: "Whenever the blood (of Christ) is being poured out (*effunditur*), it flows (*funditur*) for the forgiveness of sins." In the same way, St. John Chrysostom describes the effect of drinking from the eucharistic chalice: "This blood is the salvation of our soul; it cleanses our soul; it beautifies our soul;...it makes it shine even more than gold. Through the pouring out of this blood, it becomes possible to walk the path to heaven" (PG 59:261).

Pope St. Gregory the Great also relates the passages fol-lowing the words of consecration for the bread and the wine directly to the celebration of the Eucharist when he writes in Dial. IV, 58,

> Although He (Christ) who rose from the dead shall die no more—death no longer has power over Him—still, although He is immortal and His living form incorruptible, He is being slaughtered for us in this mysterium of the holy sacrifice (*pro nobis iterum...immolatur*).

What exactly does St. Gregory mean when he talks about the "slaughter" of the Lord? Certainly, one may surmise at this point, St. Gregory does not mean a "renewal" of the Sacrifice on the cross, since he continues, "Because there His body provides nourishment, His flesh is being divided up (*partitur*), His Blood pours out—no longer into the hands of the non-believers, but into the mouths of the believers."

According to St. Gregory, the "slaughter" of Christ occurs in the form of the sacrament when the consecrated bread is being "divided up" and the consecrated wine "poured out" into the mouths of the faithful. The direct, literal translation of the words for the consecration of the bread used during the early forms of the Roman Canon and recorded in *De sacramentis* (IV, 21) are: "This is my Body, which is being broken for you (*confringetur*)."

Similarly, St. John Chrysostom has this to say: "Why does (the Apostle) say, 'The bread which we break'? (1 Cor. 10:17). We can see this during the Eucharist, but not at the cross. Yet what He has suffered on the cross, He is suffering for you at this Sacrifice. He allows Himself to be divided, so as to nourish all (participants in the sacrifice of the Mass.)"

In conclusion then, the words of consecration for the bread and wine are associated, first and foremost, with receiving the gifts of the Eucharist—and that means receiving them here and now—and with the graces bestowed as a result of the individual receiving these gifts; the words do not primarily refer to the Sacrifice on the cross. The use of the phrase confringetur ("who is being broken") cannot possibly be associated with the death of Jesus on the cross, precisely because in the Gospel of St. John (19:32-33), it is reported that the soldiers did not break the bones of the Lord, although they did just that to the two persons who had been crucified with the Lord. Thus, the phrase *confringetur* can only relate to the breaking of the eucharistic bread, even though this act, just as the pouring out of the chalice into the mouth of the recipient, is also a symbol of the violent death of Jesus on the cross.

About the Author

Monsignor Klaus Gamber was born on April 23, 1919 in Ludwigshafen on the Rhine. He served as a soldier for six years during World War II. He was ordained a priest on June 29, 1948, in Regensburg. He devoted himself to pastoral duties, which he had to give up because of serious illness. In 1957, he co-founded and became the Director of the Institute of Liturgical Science in Regensburg, his consuming interest being the study of liturgy in the Western and Eastern Church. He remained in his post until his death on June 2, 1989, at the age of 70.

Monsignor Gamber received a doctorate in theology and was subsequently awarded an honorary doctorate in philosophy. He was made an honorary member of the Pontifical Liturgical Academy in Rome in 1958, a chaplain to the pope in 1965, and his secret chamberlain in 1966.

A Selection of the Author's Publications

Monsignor Klaus Gamber wrote or edited 361 books, articles, research papers and editions of patristic and liturgical texts. A sampling is below.

Codices liturgici latini antiquiores, University Press of Freiburg, Switzerland, 1963 and 1968.

Zeugen des Herrn. Zeugnis der Martyrer der Frühkirche nach zeitgenössischen Gerichtsakten, Briefen und Berichten (Witnesses of the Lord: The Witness Borne by the Martyrs of the Early Church based on Contemporary Court Records, Letters and Reports), Waldstadt Publishing House, Einsiedeln, Switzerland, 1962; out of print.

Liturgie übermorgen. Gedanken zur Geschichte und Zukunft des Gottesdienstes (Liturgy for the Day After Tomorrow: Thoughts about the History and the Future of Worship), Herder Publishing House, Freiburg-Basel-Vienna, 1966.

Missa Romensis. Beiträge zur frühen römischen Liturgie und zu den Anfängen des Missale Romanum (Missa Romensis: Contributions on the Subject of Early Roman Liturgy and the

Beginnings of the Missale Romanum), Friedrich Pustet Publishing House, Regensburg, 1970.

Ritus modernus. Gesammelte Aufsätze zur Liturgiereform (Ritus Modernus: Collected Essays about the Reform of the Liturgy), Friedrich Pustet Publishing House, Regensburg, 1972.

Sacrificium laudis. Zur Geschichte des frühchristlichen Eucharistiegebets (Sacrificium Laudis: About the History of the Eucharistic Prayer among the Early Christians), Friedrich Pustet Publishing House, Regensburg, 1973.

Liturgie und Kirchenbau. Studien zur Geschichte der Messfeier und des Gotteshauses in der Frühzeit (Liturgy and the Building of Churches: The History of the Celebration of Mass and of Church Buildings in the Early [Christian] Period), Friedrich Pustet Publishing House, Regensburg, 1976.

Sakramentarstudien und andere Arbeiten zur frühen Liturgiegeschichte (Studies of Sacramentaries and Other Works About the Early History of Liturgy), Friedrich Pustet Publishing House, Regensburg, 1978.

Sacrificium missae. Zum Opferverständnis und zur Liturgie der Frühkirche (Sacrificium Missae: Sacrificial Offering and the Liturgy of the Early Church), Friedrich Pustet Publishing House, Regensburg, 1980.